Craig on Theatre

Edward Gordon Craig's work is at present known more by reputation than example. A comparatively short career as actor, designer and director was characterised by projects of startling originality involving the major European theatrical figures of his day, and a regrettably small output of finished work, little of which gave him personal satisfaction. Yet it was not simply the fortunate result of his being the son of a famous actress, Ellen Terry, that he was courted in the theatres of Europe by such as Otto Brahm, Eleanora Duse, Reinhardt and Stanislavsky. The theories which he expounded in copious books and magazine articles were matched by series of woodcuts, etchings and 'stage visions', which suggested a way forward into the twentieth century for a theatre still dominated by the ideas of the nineteenth.

This book brings together for the first time a cross section of Craig's theories, demonstrating that even some of those wilder notions for which he tends to be remembered were far from the work of a mere visionary with no concept of the practicalities of the stage. Steeped though he was in the theatre of the past, he had no wish to resurrect it. Rather he looked forward to a new era when the theatre would escape from the twin strangleholds of literature and literalism. Some of those ideas have dated, others have become commonplaces of modern practice. Still more can serve as a stimulus to each new generation of stage designers and directors.

J. Michael Walton is a senior lecturer in the Drama Department at the University of Hull. After studying Classics at St Andrews and Drama at Bristol University, he went into the professional theatre and worked as an actor and director before moving to Hull in 1965. In 1972–3 he was Visiting Professor in Theatre at the University of Denver. He has directed over forty professional and student productions. His publications include articles on Chekhov, modern British theatre and the theatre of classical Athens, which is also the subject of his book *Greek Theatre Practice*.

Craig on Theatre

edited by

J. MICHAEL WALTON

457494

Methuen · London

This selection first published in 1983
by Methuen London Ltd., 11 New Fetter Lane, London EC4P 4EE

Selection, Introduction and Commentary
copyright © 1983 by J. Michael Walton
For details of copyright in the individual extracts of
Craig's writings, see Acknowledgements.

Printed in Great Britain by
Richard Clay (The Chaucer Press) Ltd, Bungay, Suffolk

ISBN 0 413 49540 X (Hardback)
 0 413 47220 5 (Paperback)

Contents

Illustrations

The sources of the photographs that appear in this book are as follows:

Gillian Jason Gallery, London – cover, 1, 10, 11, 12, 21; Nationalbibliothek, Vienna – 2, 7, 8, 9; Ohtani Women's College, Osaka, Japan – 4, 5, 6 (missing); Bibliothèque d'art et d'archéologie, Paris – 13, 14, 15, 16; Victoria and Albert Museum, London – 17, 24; Bibliothèque National, Paris – 18, 19, 20, 22, 23.

Author's Note

Craig's prose-style was as eccentric and magnetic as the man himself. His spelling too was personal, and could on occasions vary almost from paragraph to paragraph. In the name of clarity, I have taken the liberty of regularising it, though the punctuation is usually his own. Where I have edited his original words, I have attempted to do so only by removing passages which do not seem immediately germane to the argument.

Edward Gordon Craig

If you take a train to London from the North-East you pass the Gordon
Craig Theatre at Stevenage half an hour before reaching King's Cross.
The outside walls are painted brick red and yellow ochre. What Craig
might have thought of the inside I cannot say. He might at least have
been gratified that the town in which he was born chose, however
belatedly, to honour his name by dedicating its civic theatre to him.

Recognition in the country of his birth has been sporadic and grudging.
In 1903 Edward Gordon Craig, at the age of thirty-one, was elected to the
Society of Twelve, an artistic circle which included among its members
Augustus John, Lucien Pissaro and William Rothenstein, but that was on
the strength of his reputation as a painter and engraver. In 1911 several of
the same Society together with friends including Lady Gregory and W. B.
Yeats, Martin Shaw, H. G. Wells and Max Beerbohm, arranged a dinner
in his honour at the Café Royal. The invitation included the following
words: 'It is well known that the theatre in Germany, Austria and Russia
admits its debt to Craig's inspiration: his influence has, indeed, gone
deeper than most people are aware of, and much that has been accomplished of late years owes its success to Craig's impulse.

'It has been felt among many of those interested in the dignity of the
Theatre in England, that it would be a fitting thing that some definite
acknowledgement be made to Craig for his unfaltering devotion and
high aims through almost insuperable difficulties.'

Forty-seven years later Craig was made a Companion of Honour, but
he was unable, for reasons of health or finance, to attend the investiture
in London.

His reputation today is an odd one. All those with even a passing
interest in the theatre past and present know his name but most of
them for the wrong reasons. 'Wasn't he the man whose scenery looked
fine on paper but fell down as soon as it was put up?' 'Didn't he want
to do away with the actor in favour of the puppet?' 'Surely he was one
of those theorists from the turn of the century who wrote a lot but

never *did* anything. Was he really still alive in 1966?'

As with most popular fallacies such remarks represent a sad distortion of small truths. The screens for the 1912 production of *Hamlet* staged with Stanislavsky at the Moscow Art Theatre did collapse only hours before the first performance: Craig did fulminate against 'the evil tendencies of the modern theatre' and promote the cause of the Über-marionette, 'the actor plus fire, minus egoism': the last production on which he worked was Ibsen's *The Pretenders* staged in Denmark for the Poulsen brothers in 1926. He did earn his living in the theatre for the most part, however, for a good twenty years as actor, designer and director.

Many of his designs and working drawings survive. Together with a large body of writings they have served to influence practitioners, by their own admission, as diverse as Reinhardt, Stanislavsky, Meyerhold and Brecht. If the task of evaluating and comparing ideas in the arts of the last hundred years seems to have been reduced on occasions to an academic pastime, at least in Craig's case, we are dealing with a man who thought constantly of the theatre of the future and whose own assessment of his work in 1908 was that it would not come into its own until the years between 1960 and 2000. The forecast was a brave one, reinforced by Kenneth Tynan, then drama critic of *The Observer*, who visited the old man at his home near Nice in 1956:

> Although he is eighty-four years old and has published little for a quarter of a century, Gordon Craig is still several lengths ahead of the theatrical *avant-garde*. Ideas that he expounded fifty years ago, in his breathless poetic prose, are nowadays bearing fruit all over Europe.

This is even more true of the nineteen-eighties when the return of the open stage and the introduction of new fabrics and materials has renewed the art of design. Perhaps the development which would most have excited Craig, though less in the office than in its significance, is the arrival of the lighting designer as an independent artistic function-ary. Advances in micro-electronics have already made possible visual subtleties undreamed of when Craig was first talking of 'painting in light'.

Craig's affirmation of movement as a senior theatrical element has also come to fruition in seventy years that have seen dance develop from when Isadora Duncan and Nijinsky represented outposts of ec-centric decadence. Today's climate of opinion, promoted over the years by such luminaries as Rudolph Laban, Martha Graham and Merce Cunningham, has ensured the acceptance of dance at every level from dramatic experiment to examination subject.

Every generation needs reminding that the word theatre comes from the Greek for 'to see' not 'to hear'. When Craig set himself up as the champion of the visual in the theatre, he saw the need for an antidote to the phenomenon of Naturalism which advocated stage surroundings which were authentic and true-to-life. Other periods of the theatre have been dominated by spectacle, but Craig had no wish to return to any of them. Instead he sought to remind audiences of perennial theatrical values, those single images which serve for a thousand words, the associations which transcend real life while giving to that life a greater meaning. Today, with the stage experiments of the last sixty years, both physical and verbal, behind us, the modern audience can take in its stride a style of theatre which reflects the fragmentation of the contemporary world. We pay homage, if somewhat baffled homage, to the inspiration of Antonin Artaud who urged 'a concrete language of the stage': we salute the stage world of Samuel Beckett peopled by representatives of the human condition reduced to essences and memories.

Can we say that Craig knew or approved of such movements? Perhaps not. As he grew older he continued to root himself in the classics of the dramatic repertoire, and there is no indication that he ever spent time or energy on the extravagant theatre of the Dadaists and Surrealists. He did meet and admire the great Russian directors Vakhtangov, Tairov and Meyerhold, the Germans Piscator and Brecht, and late in his life another English experimental director, Peter Brook, who remarks in his book *The Empty Space*: 'There is an interesting relationship between Brecht and Craig – Craig wanted a token shadow to take the place of a complete painted forest and he only did so because he recognised that useless information absorbed our attention *at the expense of something more important*. Brecht took this rigour and applied it not only to scenery but to the work of the actor and to the attitude of the audience.'

Perhaps it is in this happy knack of inspiring others that Craig's greatness lies. I might suggest that anyone who reads his writings on the theatre, whether accepting or rejecting them, cannot help but use them as a critical yardstick. Craig was a prophet of the theatre and prophets are of little use to the neutral: so he has disciples and detractors today every bit as vehement as he encountered in the theatre of the late nineteenth and early twentieth centuries.

Craig was a member of the Terry family, whose illustrious connections with the stage continue into modern times, notably in the person of his second cousin Sir John Gielgud. Ellen Terry, Craig's mother, had been married briefly to the painter George Frederick Watts, but the marriage was not legally dissolved until many years later and both Edward and his elder sister Edith were fathered by the architect Edward William Godwin. The full name of Edward Henry Gordon Craig was not official until registered by Deed Poll in 1893, but the two children had both used Craig as a stage name ever since Edith had set eyes upon Ailsa Craig, a rock off the west coast of Scotland, when she was only fifteen.

Godwin and Ellen Terry parted company when Edward was only three, and following the divorce from Watts, Ellen married a widower Charles Wardell whose stage name was Charles Kelly. This marriage proved little more successful than her first.

It has often been noted how many of the significant figures in both art and politics suffer the irreparable loss of either home or a parent during adolescence. Craig lost two fathers in a year for Charles Kelly, though now estranged from Ellen, died in 1885, and Godwin, his real father, the following year. Indeed Craig's whole childhood was beset by the kind of insecurity, financial and emotional, which must be held responsible for his later inability to maintain stable relationships. Ellen was now Irving's leading lady and devotion needs to be rather more tangible than a working actress can supply: Craig himself recorded the horror of the large house in Longridge Road to which he was brought to live at the age of four and the topmost room in which he was left to scream himself to exhausted sleep.

The petulance, sudden fits of temper and irrationality which marked and marred his relationships with theatre managers and producers throughout his life were exaggerated by a growing persecution mania which plagued his last years with the conviction that complex plots were being laid to steal his ideas. Though most artists are prone to alternating periods of elation and gloom, Craig's overriding restlessness deprived him of any settled home until late in life. He also had the misfortune for one who combined mercurial temperament with selfishness, to be attractive to women and wandered around Europe dispensing illegitimate children like a pope bestowing benedictions. One of these, Deirdre, was one of the two children of Isadora Duncan drowned in 1913 when the car in which they were travelling plunged into the Seine. Another is Craig's biographer, Edward Craig, whose account of the life and work of his father, first published in 1968, is a model of insight and honesty.

Craig did make a number of close friends among writers, musicians and particularly artists of his time, but there can be little dispute that throughout his life he was a difficult man to deal with, both in private life and in his work. But who by choice would have shared a desert island with Ibsen or Strindberg, with Meyerhold, Artaud or even Brecht? Yet these are the makers of twentieth century theatre, and Craig belongs alongside them both as a theoretician and as an artist.

The half century up to the First World War provided such a remarkable series of scientific and social changes that it is virtually impossible to suggest what influenced whom and who what. The notion of a synthesis among differing art forms is certainly seeded in this period and, without wishing to suggest precisely what outside factors contributed to Craig's view of art, there is at least some capital to be made from placing him in the context of a number of events and personalities who may be said to have dictated the new thinking of the late Victorian and Edwardian periods.

Craig was born in 1872. Henry Irving, who was to be such an influence on Craig and of whom Craig was later to write a biography, had first appeared in *The Bells* the previous year, a performance whose power was to haunt Craig when he saw it years later. The English stage was then dominated by late melodrama with the Provinces besieged by a host of stage versions of Mrs Henry Wood's tear-jerker *East Lynne*, but the move toward realism had aready begun with the Bancroft management and Tom Robertson, author of *Caste* and *Ours*, who had died in 1871.

Abroad, more significant changes were already underway. In 1872 Chekhov was only twelve years old, Stanislavsky nine and Meyerhold was not even born, but it was already five years since Ibsen's *Peer Gynt* had lifted the theatre into a new dimension. Ibsen was now beginning to fall under the influence of the realistic mood, though *A Doll's House* was still seven years away. Strindberg was writing *Master Olaf* in that year though *Miss Julie* was not to reach the stage till Craig was sixteen. The pioneer of European Naturalism, Emile Zola, was already an established writer and 1873 saw the stage version of his novel *Thérèse Raquin*, which, though confined by the restrictions of the nineteenth century stage, is still claimed as the earliest example of stage Naturalism.

At the furthest extreme from Naturalism, Wagner was in the process of creating the Ring cycle, though Adolphe Appia, who was to idolise everything about Wagner's work except the primitive way in which it was staged, was, as yet, a child. Though so different in temperament and philosophy, Craig and Appia were to promote similar ideas on the use of light and stage space without meeting until 1914.

Not only the theatre was in a state of flux in 1872. 1859 had seen the

publication of Darwin's *The Origin of Species* promoting an explanation
of human behaviour in terms of environment and heredity. A second
challenge to the edifice of Victorian society and belief had been raised
in 1867 with the publication of the first volume of *Das Kapital* by Karl
Marx, as a follow-up to the *Communist Manifesto* which he had written
with Friedrich Engels in 1848.

Freud was no more than a boy of sixteen in 1872, but Craig's birth
happened to coincide with publication of the philosopher Friedrich
Nietzsche's *The Birth of Tragedy from the Spirit of Music*. In this book
Nietzsche traced the origin of tragedy back to the conflicting natures of
the Greek gods Apollo and Dionysus as personifications of the rational
and irrational elements in human behaviour, and undermined the
notions of Realism almost before they were born. The declaration in
his later *Thus Spake Zarathustra* that 'God is dead' was to make a
further contribution to the challenge aimed at a traditional system of
values.

It would be fanciful to make anything more of the date of Craig's
birth than to underline that he was born into a changing world. His
own disinterest, even cultivated ignorance, of politics was not unusual
in his time and even extended to an uncritical admiration for Mussolini
to whom he presented two of his books while he was living in Rapallo.
In Paris during the Occupation, internment, mercifully brief, as an alien
in Stalag 142 was to remind him of the difficulty of remaining aloof to
the world around him, a difficulty first demonstrated by the requisition
of his school in the Arena Goldoni in Florence during the First World
War.

Craig's work as a practitioner was virtually over before that first
major conflict began. His career as an actor could be said to date from
an appearance at the age of twelve as a gardener's boy when his mother
was on tour with the Irving company in Chicago. Indeed he seemed
destined to become an actor and in 1889 was accepted into the company
at the Lyceum. The next ten years saw a number of personal successes
both with Irving's company and on tour with others. He played Hamlet
for the W. S. Hardy Shakespeare company in 1894 and for Ben Greet
at the Olympia Theatre in one of Irving's old costumes two years later.
Despite this, by 1897 he had given up acting and was earning a pre-
carious living for himself and his family by designing bookplates and
selling his drawings to the London illustrated papers. It was in 1898
that he launched the first of the three magazines with which he was
closely associated, *The Page*. Though this was of limited scope and
ambition it paved the way for *The Mask* which he published and for

which he wrote most of the articles under a host of pseudonyms from 1908 until 1929 with a wartime break. He also started a magazine in 1918 called *The Marionette* in which he intended to publish his own puppet plays, but by July 1919 this enterprise had folded. *The Mask* at this time was little more than a pamphlet, but its fortunes revived and publication continued to a complete fifteen volumes.

Craig's first stage production was a charity performance of De Musset's *No Trifling with Love* as early as 1893, but his major work as a director began with productions of Purcell's *Dido and Aeneas* with Martin Shaw in 1900; *The Masque of Love*, based on a Fletcher play, in 1901; and Handel's *Acis and Galatea* the following year. In each of these the work was remembered in particular for Craig's remarkable designs and for the manipulation of the operatic choruses. A production of Laurence Housman's *Bethlehem* was followed by two productions starring his mother and underwritten by her, Ibsen's *The Vikings* at the Imperial Theatre in April 1903 and *Much Ado About Nothing* a month later. During the next ten years Craig embarked on a series of ventures, as designer and director, with some of the most celebrated names in the European theatre, Otto Brahm, Max Reinhardt, Eleanora Duse, Beerbohm Tree. Though these were frequently thwarted by clashes of interest, Craig's reputation spread, helped by the publication of *The Art of the Theatre* in 1905. This was re-published together with a further series of essays in 1911 under the title *On The Art of the Theatre* and his reputation was confirmed as a kind of *génie terrible* by the co-production with Stanislavsky of *Hamlet* which finally reached the stage in January 1912. The ideas for the production were all his and *Hamlet* marks the high point of Craig's career as a director, for all his personal misgivings about the final product.

The school for which he had campaigned for many years opened in Florence in 1913, only to close at the beginning of the war. Apart from the production of *The Pretenders* in Denmark in 1926 he did no further work within a theatre.

Retired actor at twenty-five, virtually retired director and designer by the age of forty, Craig's reputation hangs upon a small number of productions, and a host of ideas, enterprises and visions promoted in *On The Art of the Stage* and his later books, in particular *Towards a New Theatre*, *Scene*, *The Theatre Advancing*, and *Books and Theatres*, the last two of which contained many articles reprinted from *The Mask*: these and biographies of his idol, Henry Irving, and his mother, Ellen Terry, whom, Sir John Gielgud once said, 'he never forgave for not having Irving as his father'.

Today some of his ideas are no surprise at all. That is a tribute to Craig. Still more are a great surprise and that is even more of a tribute. Although his advocacy of the director as *generalissimo* is currently out of fashion, the majority of his notions on the use of light and space are a source of constant stimulus. Some of his assessments of major plays may seem distorted, but others, notably the promotion of the supernatural in *Macbeth*, provide an interpretation which has itself become a classic. For the rest, his own writings provide both promotion and apology. They are old-fashioned only in so far as the vocabulary of the theatre has grown. The ideas are as fresh as ever.

Introduction

from *Woodcuts and Some Words* (1924)

I can but count it a blessing that I meddled with wood-engraving. It may be said that had I not had the inclination for it, nor given it so much of my time, I should have been obliged to keep my nose to my own grindstone, that is to say, to the stage of a theatre.

I certainly did avoid a great deal of stage experience. For example, after 1903, had I been obliged to enter an English theatre regularly, night by night, I might have kept my hand in – I wonder! – my nose certainly would have been ground off; and after that my brains ground out, my spirit ground down by prejudice, insularity and all that was powerful in the London theatre; yet I would dearly have liked never to have had to leave the English theatre, even for a month.

Perhaps this statement needs qualifying. All the London theatres would surely not have been such tyrannical places as my words might lead you to suppose. Let me state as clearly as I can how it was that this London theatre was tyrannical to me as an artist.

First of all, it offered me no schooling. I came to the Lyceum Theatre in 1889 untrained. Irving, as I said, gave me five pounds a week at once. I assumed, as best I could, the airs which go with so large a sum, such a head-turning salary as this. That sort of thing is not discipline, that is policy – the policy of a manager. I had to get through as best I could, without much understanding and with little talent and with no training, the part of a young man, a rather central figure in a play called *The Dead Heart*. I was eighteen years old. Now who was in the theatre on the first night of this play, who of my contemporaries? Mr Max Beerbohm was one. I believe Mr Aubrey Beardsley was another. Professor Rothenstein was there too, I think. Each of these representative men of their time; one to become the greatest living illustrator, one the head of the Royal College of Art, the other the writer of the finest prose of this day. Painting, drawing and letters have standards, and are judged by them. These standards helped to make these artists. The theatre has practically no standards. The mob is allowed to shout or hiss a performance in or out of existence. Had I at that time known this, I might have chosen another field in which to work. Had I been told that my theatre, dear as it was to me, was not going to fight against the prejudice it hugged and still hugs, was going to remain insular, was content in its conceit, was taking no steps to rid itself of its folly, I think I would have done as I have just now said.

But the truth is, I was devoted to the theatre just as I am devoted to it now, and that meant not seeing one of its faults. Yet it means more than that sometimes. For I see a few of its faults clearly now, but I love it not a jot less than I did.

What I want now in the light is what I wanted then in the dark. Groping – puzzled – in the midst of will-o'-the-wisps calling from all sides, I instinctively felt adrift. Yet I was in the very first of English playhouses. There was nothing to catch hold of. There should, of course, have been a school connected with the Lyceum Theatre, a place where those who were beginners could study, could be clearly and slowly trained, directed by masters neither too pedantic nor too go-as-you-please. The only school we had was the stage of the theatre in rehearsal time and during the performances. Just as Irving paid us high salaries from policy, not from principle, so he taught us to go here, move thus, speak so and act, as any other manager does, not with the least intention of making an amazing troupe of actors, but in the hope, the despairing hope, of ever making us more than dummies. He neither showed this despair nor this hope. So that the Lyceum 'school' was the old one known as the school of experience. The school of experience is a pretty sound one if you are allowed a great quantity and variety of experiences; that is to say, if you can be in one company today, another next month, a third six months later; if the experience is always changing, if you are acting hundreds of parts before several different kinds of audiences in the course of a year, and with as many types of fellow-actors.

But to be year in and year out in the same town, with the same audience, with the same actors, acting one play, is fatal to development. If such a theatre must exist, it can only develop if it has attached to it a school; and a school which inspires, urging the younger workers forward, and which (cautious too) pulls them in – a school which instructs.

I was not yet seventy-five years old, and no one under seventy-five was allowed to have ideas at that time. It happened also that I was able to escape. This is not the sixteenth century I am writing of, nor the seventeenth, not even the eighteenth. It was the end of the nineteenth century, when little remained to the stage of its old spirit – that creative old spirit; this was in 1896, and the place was England, a place where theatres and playgoing were still considered something wrong and to write real true drama was forbidden. It was a strange period, a period when disbelief was the creed of creeds; when doubt and boredom had already eaten their way into mind and spirit of too many workers in the theatre, when time was preparing to break the old theatre. One hopes such a time is gone by.

Then it was that some few young men and women determined to save the situation. They realised that to do so they would first have to free themselves from the yoke of the theatre, its dear and heavy yoke, a yoke somehow loved because it entailed the privilege of remaining in the old house. This privilege had to be given up.

You do not here need any description of what pain is. You all know what it feels like: you know the pain in the heart. It was this we then encountered when we had to cut free from the old house – yet, I hope, did our duty.

You see, a man of twenty-five or thirty in those days really could not open his mouth except on the condition that he would repeat a catch phrase, an old lie. Originality and sincerity were banned. All was 'impossible' in those days; you might speak sense only when too old to remember what it was you had intended to say. 'Do as was done last time' was the rule, and a rule not to be broken. A fine principle, to be sure!

Only one thing was left to do, and we did it. By we I mean a few men and women, possibly four or even five: one in England, one in France, one in Germany, one in Switzerland, one in America. We were unknown to each other at the time, and so we worked independently of each other.

But we all heard the cue, all venerated the fine actors and detested the state of the theatre. What the women did I cannot say; but I know what the men did was this:

First we swore not to rest till we had made a new theatre, founded on principle not on policy. It is this new theatre we are still making. We are winning and we shall win. We have not yet won. Some there are who would ask us whether what we have done is not enough, whether to have influenced so many thousands of younger artists (and older ones too) is not sufficient victory. It is something, but you misunderstand what happened in 1900 and thereabouts if you think it was so slight a matter to us as that.

What happened was that a challenge, couched in the most paltry terms imaginable, was put before the whole theatrical body, a challenge – an ultimatum: 'Starve, or do as is always done.' It is paltry in theatrical folk, over-comfortable in their day of success, to challenge the right of the younger brains to wake up the theatre if they can. These same comfortable ones did all they could to prevent our bringing to the theatre of Europe a fresh lease of life, while continuing the policy of 'Do as was done last time.'

It was so paltry that one was bound to remark it; and so it came about that we swore not to rest until their tenth-rate rule over our ancient home was rendered futile. It is almost futile now. And we look to the young men and women of today and tomorrow to see the work finished.

It was then that I came to practise more thoroughly the craft of wood-engraving, or wood-cutting, whichever be the correct term. I found that it was a blessing to be able to turn to this rather difficult craft; teach myself through its slow ways how to design scenes and how to delineate characters better than I could do in 1896, and how to keep from heart-break, and this it did teach me. It is a work which I found allowed one to listen, if not to speak, while practising it. So I would listen to the novels of Dumas as I worked; and I was wood-cutting some three days out of seven, and listening to Dumas, and planning how to wake up the old theatre.

1. Theatre Past

Craig's abiding concern that drama had been allowed to become a province of literature was given its most eloquent and paradoxical expression in connection with Shakespeare. He dearly loved the plays. They inspired some of his most striking visions while always seeming so complex as to defy successful production. 'Literary' Theatres was a single shot in a prolonged battle but in it he states his case with defiant clarity.

The latter years of The Mask saw Craig still writing under pseudonyms – in their bibliography Ifan Kyrle Fletcher and Arnold Rood list sixty-six – but concentrating on aspects of theatre history. For the thunder and the passion one must look to the earlier volumes written before the First World War. Then it was that the reforming zeal first led him to look at the great periods of the past and to promote a new theatre built on strengths recreated, or rather rediscovered. He saw no point in attempting to reconstruct the Athenian or Elizabethan theatres. He looked instead for new ways forward which would acknowledge and build upon the best of the past, at both literary and sub-literary levels. Writing of The Perishable Theatre he identified those aspects of theatre which Peter Brook in The Empty Space chose, sixty years later, to call 'the rough theatre'.

Being a graphic artist and engraver Craig came easily to appreciate the pedigree and virtues of mask and puppet, but he found inspiration in any aspect of earlier theatre which had succeeded in capturing the soul and imagination of the onlooker. Those periods appealed most which had thrown up a wide variety of audience compelled not only by intellectual concern and social obligation. Not that the theatre of classical Athens, to which Craig regularly referred, disavowed intellect and the political, but what he recognised in it was a drama rooted in theatrical image and theatrical truth, which was able only incidentally to stand up to linguistic and structural analysis. It was eminently suitable that he should not only be attracted to classical tragedy, but also give it his most eloquent approbation by means of the Black Figures, a bas-relief series which he began in 1907. Close in form to the Javanese *wayang klitik*, the figures were not puppets but self-standing, 'solid' silhouettes no more than a foot in height. Not all of the series was black. Some were white wood and several related to the plays of Shakespeare rather than the Greeks. But the Greek and Roman figures are the most convincing, encapsulating, as they do, the notion of masked acting [see illustrations 10, 11, 12].

A Note on Masks puts the case for the mask as a dramatic weapon not in emulation of the classical tradition but for its intrinsic merit. O'Neill, Brecht and Shaffer have been among those who have shown new ways in which the mask can regain a place of honour within a twentieth-century tradition.

It is typical of Craig that in the same essay on masks he should deplore the fact that the mask has degenerated to the level of the dance and the marionette, when he can elsewhere enthuse with equal fervour over both these modes of dramatic expression. *Gentlemen, The Marionette* celebrates the string puppet. The new magazine founded after the Great War was called *The Marionette* and contained the text of puppet plays he had written. Writing in 1912 he was well aware of how readily critics had latched onto the idea of the Über-marionette and wilfully misinterpreted it. Even in retrospect, however, it is difficult not to have some sympathy with an acting profession and a public so berated.

The essay on *Candlelight* concludes this section, written rather later than the others. Craig's study of the theatre of the past was comprehensive. There was also something of the buccaneer about him, something of the border raider. He plundered the past systematically, all periods, all fashions, to provide a foundation for his 'new' theatre. Others were to follow his lead, notably the great Russian directors, to many of whom the theatre of the fairground and market-place represented a kind of Eldorado.

Craig roamed further than any of them. Balanced, if anything about Craig can claim to be balanced, against this admiration for simple theatricality was an affinity with high artifice. Combined, they worked to the heart of things. Electric light was still a new toy in the theatre of the turn of the century. Craig was certainly among the first to recognise that its overriding potential lay in close control. He could also claim to have brought a painter's eye to the theatre, considering the atmospheric of the stage to be dependent less on a dimming-down of the maximum than on a fading-up from the minimum. The sense of mood lives in every stage design he created.

'Literary' Theatres (1908)

Those people who are interested at all times in creating a 'literary theatre' would do well to remember the dangers which beset such unnatural efforts. Unfortunate has been the end of all such attempts.

For nearly thirty years Goethe struggled in conjunction with Schiller to create for the Germans a new theatre. Although Goethe was more than a poet, he was first a poet, and everything else in him kept time to the words which he sang. He set out to create a literary stage; he would not have it that the stage should be, as he rather weakly calls it, 'the reflection of natural life in amusing mirrors'. And so he marshalled his army of words – all of them to assault the theatre – stood in the midst and watched his veritable Thirty Years' War, his battle of words against visions, sacked the theatre, razed it to the ground, and then, scanning the horizon, was surprised that the theatre was no more to be seen. In fact, even he, the greatest man of his age, utterly fails to understand what the art of the theatre might be.

And now there are others, if not the greatest men of their age, talented in great measure, who court the same failure in attempting this impossible and fantastic thing.

I should have thought the artists would understand the charming separation which must ever exist between the arts. I have no fear for the theatre: I do not believe it can suffer any harm even by an assault such as that made upon it by Goethe; but wishing to see less confusion in the public mind as to what the art of the theatre is and what it is not, I must ever protest against the unnecessary deception of the public in this, to me, most important matter.

When literary men shall be content and patient enough to study the art of the theatre as an art separate from the art of literature, there will be nothing to prevent us from welcoming them into the house.

The Perishable Theatre (1921)

When speaking of the perishable theatre I do not want anybody to imagine that I use the word 'perishable' as implying something hardly worth consideration. I use it so as to distinguish it from the durable theatre, to place it apart; not that it is inferior to the durable theatre, only that it is different.

Neither would I like my readers to imagine that by a perishable theatre I mean the present theatre.

As an aid to imagining such a theatre one needs but to recall the different periods of theatrical art, to seize upon those parts which are least stable, most evanescent; picture them more unstable, more evanescent, and we have an idea of the thing.

And now, let us consider it in the same order as we did the durable theatre.

First, the drama.

All would have to be spontaneous. If it were a play of words it would have to be improvisation. If dancing, very much 'go as you please', as in the folk dances; if singing, it would have to be improvised too; in the cases of spoken play and sung play, or opera, we have plenty of precedent to go upon. In Italy in the fifteenth and sixteenth centuries they were masters of the art of improvisation, and, as a proof of how perishable this improvisation was, there is really little more than the comedy of Molière which records it; and in Molière of course the dialogue is highly polished and finished, brought almost to a durable state.

To some extent we find a light form of the perishable play in the vaudeville performances of today. I have said 'light', and refrained from saying 'inferior', for the good reason that I do not think them inferior. If those who question this will try to improvise even to the extent that the vaudevillists do, they will find it such a difficult task that I think they will change their minds if ever tempted to dub it 'inferior'.

We find a considerable amount of improvisation in the circus also, at least in the old-fashioned circuses – newly furbished up as they may be – that we meet with in Europe. I do not know what those are like that one meets with in America, but imagine they can do as well in their improvising bouts.

I have taken the trouble now and then hurriedly to write down the conversation between the clowns in a circus, and to a great extent it resembles the conversation in Molière; in essentials the method is practically the same, but when recorded the result is anything but funny. The point made at the end is always the thing on which they are counting to convulse their hearers, and the rest is all preparation to get them into an expectant state of mind.

I myself have never heard any singers improvise, but I have heard some instrumentalist musicians who roam about the streets of Florence in the spring and summer evenings who do improvise, and sometimes do it well enough to convince any unbeliever that such a thing is not an impossibility.

I think it is unnecessary to mention the East when speaking of the possible development of Western art; not that I am wanting in respect for what the East possesses and can produce; but there is a danger in becoming too early acquainted with a matured foreign development of an art which should be evolved afresh from one's own soil.

After working for many years and searching for ways and means to create what at last comes clearer into vision each day, one can with more safety venture into the East to gain encouragement and assistance. But for the present we will leave it out of the discussion, although doubtless improvisation is practised continually in many parts of Asia.

I think that those who improvise dramas should limit themselves to light subjects which they do not mind losing; to improvise on the theme of Romeo and Juliet, or Coriolanus, or Julius Ceasar, or the Pharaohs, would seem to be out of tune; probably this is why clowns unconsciously select themes of robbing their neighbours, or making them fall over a hidden wire, these petty assaults being things that can be forgotten as soon as done; but the murder of Julius Caesar or the burial of one of the Pharaohs is not a thing that any seriously flippant man would wish to forget in a hurry. For my part, although it is a digression to say so, I think that only a flippantly serious man would select such themes for the durable theatre either. How rightly they belong to the present-day theatre, which is neither durable nor ephemeral!

Although the main theme of the comic improvisators is 'doing' another man, the incidents are varied and the by-paths many. And the moral of the whole is always good, for it is the fool who pretends to be wiser than the other fool who invariably gets 'done', because he wishes to show his superior wisdom.

It is seldom elegant, this comedy, and yet a perishable theatre would have to possess its improvised dramas that were elegant and even exquisite. Perhaps here we should drop speech and pass to the dance, care being taken to avoid anything like a dance of a priestess before the altar of love, lest the little boy in the corner should giggle – through good taste.

But dances based upon the movements of the perishable things in nature – the ugly little insects and the more beautiful insects; in fact the whole short-lived creation; and, perhaps, the passing phases of childhood; even the brittleness of toys suggests itself as a theme. Not only the fact that a thing is perishable, but that it is mutable is of value.

A Note on Masks (1910)

Almost all the things which were held as essential in the theatre of the

ancients have so degenerated to the ludicrous that it is impossible to
speak of them without evoking laughter – laughter in the common
people, and a particular kind of bored drawl in many of the cultured. It
seems to me that I shall never forget trying to explain to a certain
Doctor T_____ that a piece of work which a friend of mine had just
invented for the theatre was to be given without the use of words. He
would not allow (I remember his gravity) that a serious subject should
be treated on the stage without words. And when I explained in what
way my friend had resolved to do this, how strange was the tone in
which Doctor T_____ shot out the one word, 'Ah, pantomime!'

Dancing, pantomime, marionettes, masks; these things so vital to the
ancients, all essential parts of their respected art of the theatre at one
time or another, have now been turned into a jest.

Dancing – a straight toe like an icicle, strapped in like a *Cambino* in
an over-pink tight; something on the top of it like a power-puff, and
the whole thing set whirling at an enormous rate like a teetotum; it is
the modern public dancer – or when it be not this, it is in every case,
and I make no exception, merely a parody of the magic of Isadora
Duncan.

Or two persons like bears hugging one another, and slowly and heavily
as bears growling their way round a room, plod, wriggle, plod, bump;
bump, kick; this is the modern private dancer. And it is permitted.

These things being permitted and being so obviously ridiculous (even
for a ridiculous age), and being labelled as the dance, it stands to reason
that when the word 'dance' is mentioned seriously, one of these two
ridiculous pictures is conjured up by the listener. Indeed, people are
even prevailed upon to smile on reading in the Bible that King David
danced among the women before the ark. They picture to themselves a
fancy King David attired either as a powder puff or as a fox, trotting,
whirling, or lumbering around on a dusty road – probably up-hill. Why,
the thing is inconceivable! It is of no use for Royal Academicians to
draw pictures of the famous artist-king as sedately advancing with a
harp in his hands like a courtier of the time of Louis XIV. Here again
the thing is become inconceivable because sad and ridiculous; and as
the imagination of man, owing to industrialism, is not very brilliant, it
stands to reason that people give up the idea of serious and beautiful
dancing as having really existed in daily life, and fall back into the
modern distortion.

The case is even worse with pantomime. At best the world conceives
of pantomime to be what the French actors are so good at, and at the
worst they think it is Clown and Pantaloon. French actors are charming

and delightful; Clown and Pantaloon are entrancing; but these are undoubtedly not the best exponents of the art of pantomime.

So if you point to the case of Buddha teaching symbolic gesture or 'pantomime' to his pupils, the world will instantly think of Harlequinade or 'L'Enfant Prodigue', and dressing Buddha (in their mind's eye) in coloured, diamond-patterned tights, or the loose white costume of Pierrot, will giggle as they try to be serious about it all.

The marionette, too; speak of him in good society, even in learned society, and there will be an awkward moment or two. It seems that he has became one of those things that one must not mention; like the novels of Dumas, he is only for boys and girls; and if you remind any one that he figured in the Feast of Bacchus when the Egyptians celebrated those rites, people will instantly think of a poor doll tied to a stick, and resembling nothing so much as Aunt Sally. If you remind people of what M. Anatole France writes of these strange and wonderful beings, the marionettes, they will probably put M. Anatole France down as an eccentric gentleman. Still, let us hear what he says:

> J'ai vu deux fois les marionnettes de la rue Vivienne, et j'y ai pris un grand plaisir. Je leur sais un gré infini de remplacer les acteurs vivants. S'il faut dire toute ma pensée, les acteurs me gâtent la comédie. J'entends les bons acteurs. Je m'accommoderais encore des autres! Mais ce sont les artistes excellents, comme il s'en trouve à la Comédie Française, que décidément je ne puis souffrir. Leur talent est trop grand: il couvre tout. Il n'y a qu'eux.

And again:

> J'en ai déjà fait l'aveu, j'aime les marionnettes, et celles de M. Signoret me plaisent singulièrement. Ce sont des artistes qui les taillent; ce sont des poètes qui les montrent. Elles ont une grâce naïve, une gaucherie divine de statues qui consentent à faire les poupées, et l'on est ravi de voir ces petites idoles jouer la comédie.... Ces marionnettes rassemblent à des hieroglyphes Egyptiens, c'est-à-dire, à quelque chose de mystérieux et de pur, et, quand elles représentent un drame de Shakespeare ou d'Aristophane, je crois voir la pensée du poète se dérouler en caractères sacrés sur les murailles d'un temple.

And finally:

> Il y a une heure à peine que la toile du *Petit Théâtre* est tombée sur le groupe harmonieux de Ferdinand et de Miranda. Je suis sous le charme et, comme dit Prospero, 'je me ressens encore des illusions de cette île.' L'aimable spectacle! Et qu'il est vrai que les choses exquises, quand elles sont naïves, sont deux fois exquises.

Thus dancing, pantomime and the marionette, three essentials of the old dramatic art, have been allowed to go to seed, and people wonder why the dramatic art of today is so indifferent in quality, and the professors explain it by talking much about the dramatic characterisation, logic of construction, three unities, and so forth, and quote from Brunetière, Edmund Burke, and other wise men who study the moon by looking at it in deep wells.

And then the mask, that paramount means of dramatic expression, without which acting was bound to degenerate!

Used by the savages when making war at a time when war was looked upon as an art; used by the ancients in their ceremonies when faces were held to be too weak, too slight, an element; used by those artists of the theatre, Aeschylus, Sophocles and Euripides; found essential to their highest drama by the Japanese masters of the ninth and fourteenth centuries; rejected later on in the eighteenth century by the European actors, and relegated by them to the toy-shop and the fancy-dress ball, the mask has sunk to the level of the dance, of pantomime and of the marionette. From being a work of art carved in wood or ivory, and sometimes ornamented with precious metals or precious stones, and later made in leather, it has frittered itself away to a piece of paper, badly painted or covered with black satin.

I shall not here deal historically with the mask, for it is my particular wish not to divert the reader from the point at issue, which is the importance of the mask to the life of the theatre of *today* and of *tomorrow*. It is as important now as it was of old, and is in no way to be included among the things we have to put aside as old-fashioned — must in no way be looked upon merely as a curiosity, for its existence is vital to the art of the theatre.

The historical study of this question will only assist those who already perceive the value and importance of reviving in the theatre the famous and beautiful vitality of its earlier days. To those who know nothing of this value the historical study of the mask is useless, for, like the dealer in antiques, they will but collect material for the sake of collecting, and any old thing, provided it be of good craftsmanship and excessively rare, will attract them.

I have spoken and written in praise of the mask over and over again. I see the gain to the theatre which is attached to this thing. What I tell is not new; it is what all artists know.

Human facial expression is for the most part worthless, and the study of my art tells me that it is better, provided it is not dull, that instead of six hundred expressions, but six expressions shall appear upon the face of the performer. Let us take an example:

The judge sits in judgement upon the prisoner, and he shall display but two expressions, each of which is in just proportion with the other. He has two masks, and on each mask is one main *statement*, these statements being tempered by *reflections* — the hopes and fears of not merely the judge, but of justice and injustice.

Drama which is not trivial, takes us *beyond reality* and yet asks a human face, the realest of things, to express all that. It is unfair.

It is this sense of being beyond reality which permeates all great art. We see it in the little clumsily painted pictures of those periods when the true *beyond* was of more importance than a right perspective, when the perspective of thought and feeling held first place. We see it in the marvellous little Etruscan figures of but an inch high — one faces me as I write — a tiny little piece of bronze, charged with an overwhelming spirit, but which would be refused at the Royal Academies of today because, alas! its hand is as big as its head, and the toes of the foot are not defined; because it does not wriggle itself into a pose, but is poised with firm conviction — conviction, a thing detested by committees, and hence refused admission to the academies which are governed by committees.

Masks carry conviction when he who creates them is an artist, for the artist limits the statements which he places upon these masks. The face of the actor carries no such conviction; it is over-full of fleeting expression — frail, restless, disturbed and disturbing. It once would have seemed doubtful to me whether the actor would ever have the courage to cover his face with a mask again, having once put it aside, for it was doubtful whether he would see that it would serve as any gain. But now the time gives it proof, for the cinematograph favours the art of the theatre in that it reduces the number of theatres year by year.

The mask will return to the theatre; of that I grow ever more and more assured; and there is no very great obstacle in the way, although there is some slight danger attached to a misconception of its revival and a mishandling of its powers.

First of all it is not the Greek mask which has to be resuscitated; rather is it the world's mask which is going to be created. There is something very depressing in the idea of groping eastwards among ruins for the remains of past centuries. It is a great trade today, but not for the purposes of the theatre. They dig for the marbles and the bronzes and the statuettes; they unearth tombs; they rummage even for crinolines of 1860; they admire these things.

The theatre may admire the old Greek masks, and those of Japan and India, of Africa and America, but it must not dig in the ground for them; it must not collect them to copy them; it must not waste what power it has as a creator in attending to its fads; it must not play the antiquary.

That such a danger as this exists and needs guarding against is most evident. Some time ago, we do not know how far back (the collector knows), the world became tired of creating and took unto itself the rage for the old-fashioned.

'Pictures! Away with the young painters: let us fill our houses with the old paintings: drag them out of the churches, dig them out of the niches, peel them off the walls: get splendid prices for 'em: what does it matter? Hateful young men! Lovely old masters!

'Sculpture! Quick, fly to Greece! Now's the time! Nobody's looking – occupied with affairs – no money in the country, a lot of money in the ground; dig it all up; let sculpture go to the dogs, and let the old remains come back from Athens to fill our collections.

'Music! Some young musician wants his symphony played. Nonsense, costs too much; have discovered splendid new piece in little old shop for one fife and a drum; never heard anything like it before! Wonderful discovery! Tell the young man to take up chemistry.'

This craze for the antique has become a general habit, and the more antique the more the craze. Old furniture, houses packed with old furniture; old books, tapestries, all sorts of seedy metal work, even down to coins – though here the one true collector, the millionaire, is careful to keep as modern as he can. And this love of the antique is growing, so that today it is positively eating into the very people themselves, and they are becoming as antique as that which they collect, with this difference, that the old stuff has still some life in it and they have none.

This love of the antique has come into the theatre now and then; it entered into England with William Poel and his Elizabethan Stage Society. Those who know Mr Poel know him to be a man of distinction, cultivated, and an authority upon the stage of the sixteenth century. But what is that for the purpose of the living theatre? All of us feel that those connected with the stage should be distinguished and culti-vated, and authorities on all questions pertaining to the stage; but they should possess that only as a basis, and on that basis they should build anew and not merely exhibit the basis itself, saying 'Lo, the ruins of the sixteenth century! Tickets sixpence; plan of excavations, twopence extra.'

There have been others besides Mr Poel. There have been the re-vivalists of the so-called Greek theatre – a dreadful thing entirely in

Greek. Those, too, who reproduced almost a facsimile of the mediaeval theatre: a group in Russia did this.

It would be a sad thing, therefore (as all resuscitation in art is so worthless), if masks, sham-Greek in idea and modern in their quality, should be brought into the theatre, appealing only to the curious by creating a subject for small talk. No! The mask must only return to the stage to restore expression – the visible expression of the mind – and must be a creation, not a copy.

There is a second danger – the danger of the innovator. As art must not be antique, neither can it be up-to-date. I think it is Whistler who points out that art has no period whatever. It has only vitality or affectation, and under 'affectation' come both the imitation of the antique and the up-to-date, what is today well called 'the latest thing'.

The vitality of an art depends upon its artists and their willingness to work under the laws which have ruled their art from the commencement. Not laws put down by committees to suit a period, but the commandments unspoken and uninscribed – that nice law of balance which is the heart of perfect beauty, and from which springs freedom, that freedom which we hope and believe is the soul of truth. To move incessantly towards this truth is the aim of artists, and those of the theatre must not lag behind.

As has been said many times before, this will be nothing new. I have said it is what the men of the theatre began thousands of years ago; it is what the men of the theatre relinquished a few hundred years ago as beyond their strength. When we shall resume this we shall not be merely repeating; it will be no echo of a past century; the spirited reticence and passionate desire which led men to use the mask in past ages should be the same now that it ever was, and should never die. It is such an inspiration as this that we should turn to and in which we should trust. Therefore let no one attempt to put this thing on one side into the antique shop, or on to the other as an eccentric explosion of Futurism. I anticipate that the public will of course be warned by those who have thought about it for the first time and see nothing but folly in the idea of the mask as a possible proposition.

'And why do you trouble about the public and what it thinks?' I heard a cultivated man ask.

'Why, sir? Because it is not the cultured alone for whom the theatre cares, but for just those others – the public – who have been left out in the cold by the other arts; for the artists of poetry, painting, and so forth often hold the public to be too vulgar ever to love their poems and pictures, and sweep them aside with the one word, "Philistines!" '

These we (if I may speak for my fellow artists in the theatre) care for. We are not eager to go our journey without them. We need their attention and interest, their sympathy and delight if possible, and, above all, their comradeship. They need not fear that we shall ask them to sport a mask – but they must just see how it becomes us – and what fun and what fancy we can make within its shadow. Now do not be cross with us – do not trouble yourselves – show us a little sympathy; it becomes you, as our masks become us.

Gentlemen, The Marionette! (1912)

He has been waiting so long in the servants' hall that I am sure you will not find fault with me for having called him upstairs and brought you together.

Yes, he has a capacity for waiting – a talent not without charm in so humble a creature.

Humility is only an assumption in men.

Let me begin by saying a word on the nature of the marionette.

He will wait anywhere for any length of time – hidden in a box – in a cellar – or even in a century. But he will wait – and when he is brought forward and is made to feel at home he will still wait; then he waits upon you and all of us like a true servant.

There is only one actor – nay, one man – who has the soul of the dramatic poet, and who has ever served as true and loyal interpreter of the poet. This is the marionette. So let me introduce him to you.

Some of you will think you have met him before. But how is that possible? For once to meet him is never to forget him – whereas you and he are strangers.

Yet I am not entirely just. There are times when you have come across him unawares. He has many disguises, and he impersonates known heroes and despised persons equally well.

You have come across him in some deserted cathedral in Italy or even in England – for cathedrals are free and 'open to the public', and are therefore deserted. There you will have seen him hanging upon the Cross. And many Christians love him; he is interpreting the drama of the poets – man and God.

Or you have caught a glimpse of him in some temple in the Far East, enacting a more serene drama – seated before incense – hands folded – very calm.

Or in the arms of a child you have seen him, interpreting the little hearts and the larger dreams of love!

These attempts of his to reach you have not entirely failed; but still for all this until now you have actually and unconsciously kept him waiting in the servants' hall.

Gentlemen – the marionette!

Yet silently he waits until his master signals him to act, and then in a flash, and in one inimitable gesture, he readjusts the injustice of justice, the illegality of the law, the tragic farce of 'religions', the broken pieces of philosophies, and the trembling ignorance of politics.

And what other virtues can I name beside these two of silence and obedience? I think these are enough.

For his chief virtue springs out of these. Because of them he has been able to avoid that appalling crime of exhausting the stock. Born of wood, of ivory, of metal or what you will, he is content to obey his nature – their nature. He does not *pretend* to be flesh and blood. Others can be as great as he – true, he always leaves much to be desired; a great being therefore – greater than Wagner and the other celebrated men who leave nothing we long to have any longer.

After Richard Wagner, after Michelangelo, after Shakespeare – what? Blanks! They exhausted their gift, they squandered their talent; nothing was left. They did everything, suggested nothing; and their sons inherited empty purses, empty veins; instead of thinking of their responsibilities these great exhausters thought only of themselves. They were all full-stops to short sentences.

This is not the ideal of the artist, nor the ideal of mankind.

The ideal is more companionable, more paternal, gentler. It ends nothing; it will not go alone; it takes its sons with it; and it has something more priceless than all else to hand out to them at the end of the journey.

Leonardo was such an ideal. The marionette is another.

The marionette, through his two virtues of obedience and silence, leaves to his sons a vast inheritance. He leaves to them the promise of a new art.

The marionette is a little figure, but he has given birth to great ones who, if they preserve the two essentials, obedience and silence, shall preserve their race. The day that they hunger for further power they shall surely fall.

These children of his I have called Über-marionettes, and have written of them at some length.

What the wires of the Über-marionette shall be, what shall guide him, who can say? I do not believe in the mechanical, nor in the material. The wires which stretch from divinity to the soul of the poet are wires which might command him. Has God no more such threads to spare – for one more figure? I cannot doubt it.

I will never believe anything else.

And did you think when I wrote five years ago of this new figure who should stand as the symbol of man – and when I christened him the Über-marionette – to see real metal or silken threads?

I hope that another five years will be long enough for you to draw those tangleable wires out of your thoughts.

1920

I see now it will run into ten – or eleven.

ALEXANDER HEVESI ON MARIONETTES (1908)

To the pupils in my dramatic college I put the following question yesterday: 'Do you consider the marionette natural?' 'No.' They answered with one voice.

'What!' I replied indignantly. 'Not natural? All its movements speak with the perfect voice of its nature. If a machine should try to move in imitation of human beings, that would be unnatural. Now follow me: the marionette is more than *natural*; it has style – that is to say, *unity of expression*; therefore the marionette theatre is the true theatre.'

Candlelight (1922)

In 1733 on 2 May 'Il Sirio' is produced at Bologna in the Teatro Malvezzi.

It is performed until 21 June, and during that time twenty-six times. The music is by Hasse, the libretto by Metastasio. Francesco Bibienz (Galli) designs the last scene – for which he is paid 200 lire italiano, 995 lire being spent on cloth – wood – colours – woodwork, etc., and 434 lire to assistant painters; 1,548 lire is paid for the illumination, candles and oil on the stage and in the auditorium. The total expense for twenty-six performances is 31,572 lire. The takings are 26,468 lire: Loss, 5,104 lire.

Candles – oil – it sounds very untidy. But we lose so much when we want everything as we have it now, and fail to understand that many a thing as it was then, was excellent, ... and so different from what we suppose.

To our eyes it does not seem a pretty thing to see the pale white candles dripping their grease from high chandeliers, nor the spluttering wicks of oil lamps, smoking when not spluttering. But we have only to exert our imagination a little to reconstruct the real sight.

If 150 candles in the glare of our modern light look pale and greasy, they look nothing of the kind when in the delicate rays of their own light.

I am fond of much light, and so, as I write this, I sit in a room which burns 200 candle-power's worth of light, . . . possibly 250. It is a small room so I am wasting the light.

And it glares, – yet I have veiled the lamps with shades. Still it is a glare. I like it. Darkness, except in some cases, is horrible to me. And where is darkness good? In what kind of room? A rich one. My room is a plain one, and that is like most modern rooms: the more light in it the richer it will feel. But in the eighteenth century and the seventeenth the rooms were rich as rich could be. The salons, bedrooms, passages, all bristled with points which caught every ray of light. The ceilings alone were marvels of carving, gilded and coloured, which acted as reflectors to the candlelight. What wasn't a looking-glass was a lustre; what not a lustre, a spangle.

It is this which made candles right. This, and the darkness which also was *rich*; for gold – burnished – is as rich in its gloom as in its glitter.

At night open some door which leads into a seventeenth- or eighteenth-century room gilded or silvered, and strike a match. The place will seem to go off like a firework.

Come into some chaste room devised by the puritanical mind and strike a match there, and the only suggestion of life we receive is something like that which a drowning man receives as he sinks lower and lower in the sea.

The gilt room is, you may think, the error of nabobs; the other is, perhaps, the achievement of nobobs.

And now consider what a theatre looked like in the seventeenth and eighteenth centuries with some few hundred candles to light the whole building, – stage, scenes, passages, auditorium and staircases. . . .

But I run up these staircases too quickly. People were more leisurely in those days. One single oil lamp at each turn to a staircase of a theatre, and that was all. Three turns, three lamplets, . . . like those in churches, possibly placed in lanthorns securely locked with padlocks. I need hardly say 'possibly', for they most certainly would have to be locked, bolted and barred to remain unstolen.

Up the staircase then – down a passage – the passage which circles the theatres and is behind the boxes; ten lamps in each long curving passage . . . flickering.

We knock on the door of Box 13 and it is opened at once. We enter and make a sixth and seventh . . . for you mustn't go. 'This is my friend, Ferdinando Galli – this is his wife – this his son Antonio – and this Guiseppe – and this is Maria who cooks a *Pollo alla Cacciatore* better than anyone could imagine.'

'This is the editor of *Current Opinion* . . . Mr Parker. Parker wants to know, Ferdinando, why the passages are so dark and the staircases so dreadful.' . . .

Ferdinando never replies to a silly question, but Mrs Ferdinando does. She is a most lively lady and very pleasant mannered . . . thank God without being brilliant. 'We are never brilliant here in Bologna,' she says pleasantly, turning to Mr Parker as though she had read my thoughts. 'Do you find these four chandeliers give too little light?' she asked, making Parker sit down by her.

To Mrs Galli, Parker said he found it very pleasant – and, quite puzzled that Ferdinando would not give him so much as a word, he determined to force it from him. . . . 'Say, Buddy,' said he, pulling up his chair close to Ferdinando so that the rest of us had to squeeze against the walls, 'are you enjoying yourself here?'

This was not what the master had expected, and it therefore refreshed him. – 'Say, Buddy,' went on Mr Parker, pointing to the stage, 'can you see a darn thing out there?'

The truth is – (I have to say it – for Ferdinando never opened his lips that evening) – the truth is my friend Parker of the twentieth century was so tuned up to a theatre containing 6,000 candle-power light in the auditorium and another 15,000 candle-power light on the stage that he couldn't bear what he took for darkness.

Now Ferdinando and the rest of us there were of the eighteenth century and had come from our houses at about six o'clock while it was still fairly light, and as it grew darker had entered the Teatro Malvezzi, had waited twenty minutes in the Caffè del Teatro downstairs where it is rather lighter than outside, had gradually come upstairs – had strolled into our loggia . . . while the chandeliers were being lighted, and had seen them stop spinning: all this had brought a gradual increase of light to us, so that by the time the curtain rose the addition of sixty to sixty-five candles on the stage almost made day for us.

Then I had been called away suddenly by this good Parker, who had sent me a note to say he had only three more hours to spend in Bologna, at which city he had but just arrived; I from politeness to him had slipped quietly out of the box – sped down to the caffè – round by the arcades – in and out of the pillars sought for him furiously – and at last found him, or rather been found by him as he arrived, calm as death,

after having 'run round to see the Santa Petronus' while waiting for me
to come down 365 metres from my loggia.

'What makes you bury yourself here?' says he as greeting.

I like Parker's journal. *Current Opinion* recalls the *Review of Reviews*
which Stead started in London, only it's livelier . . . I mean more glare
. . . the lights turned on full . . . awfully jolly. One gets all the news one
wants to get and one is grateful one gets it four weeks late . . . for
Current Opinion is a monthly journal.

This getting it late tones it down. Like a shade over a lamp – like
distance from the view. And so when Parker brought me up with a jerk
asking me what made me bury myself in Bologna – I had felt I wanted
a whole month to answer that question – to state the whole facts of the
case, to put in the shadows and the high lights, – and I had thought,
'Anyhow Ferdinando will answer him,' and the thought had made me
smile so pleasantly at him that he had taken me by the arm and dragged
me up to an oil lamp to get the full flow of my geniality.

Now a single oil lamp sends a strong shadow into those places which
are hollow and lights up all bony parts: and Parker had looked really
rather theatrically distressed as he shook his head and again said, 'You're
burying yourself alive here.'

'What will he think of Ferdinando?' I had thought; for Ferdinando
is nearly all bone; – but I had cheered up at the thought of what
Ferdinando would *say* – and how brilliant he would be.

So it was terrible to me when Ferdinando refused to utter a word . . .
refused to make European fireworks or even an ordinary show – and
Parker had only another two hours left; – had to go to his hotel – eat
something – pack – and catch the train; – and indeed, when I looked
round a minute later Parker was gone . . . blown out as it were.

Ferdinando then said with deliberation and a pause between each
word: '*Ecco un uomo che è morto, e non se ne dà per inteso,*' or in plain
American, 'That is a man who is dead and doesn't know it.' The phrase
later on was carried to America where it went into common use, but it
was never used again quite in the same sense as Ferdinando had used it.

.   .   .   .   .   .

The lights in the Malvezzi Theatre and in the San Cassiano in Vene-
zia were sufficient. They were soft, well-placed and reflected from the
gold that was everywhere (on the dresses even) – from the lustres and
the looking-glasses, from the sparkling fans, and from the thousands of
spangles which in the evening found their way, in those days, on to
everything and gave a glow and a sparkle against colour that was rich.

The face stood out.

Nowadays, by the use of too much light, we have probably forced the use of too much black in clothes, in woodwork, in carpets, in seats, . . . and against all this our faces stand out, not as of old, but like dried white figs or like paper.

It is quite necessary, all this glare in theatres, because there is a glare in the streets at night and a glare in our houses too. And, leaving these, we have to be met by a greater glare or we grow depressed.

No art is used at all . . . anywhere.

This is what I had to say about lighting.

It is not much – but it's more than Ferdinando said to Parker.

2. Theatre Present and Future

'Public taste was never better than it's going to be tomorrow' has a fine Craigian ring to it. Disenchanted with the theatre of his own time, Irving excepted, Craig took every opportunity to lambast the English theatre for refusal to take risks, risks being identified for the most part with employing Craig himself on his own terms. Not even he would have denied that there was a risk in so doing but, as he replied to the objection that his setting for Bach's *Matthew Passion* would cost too much, 'Not to do it will cost much more.'

The critical success of the small number of his English productions in the early years of the century promoted his ideas far beyond the audiences who witnessed them. Backed by his own writings, in particular *The Art of the Theatre* first published in 1905, and the designs, many of which appeared in commemorative programmes, Craig found himself by his early thirties something of a celebrity in the European theatre before ever working there. Such a state of affairs was soon amended as offers to direct or design flooded in from leading lights of the continental theatre. If Craig's temperament ensured that even the most fruitful collaborations were periodically soured by argument and recrimination, he found enough in the Moscow Art Theatre and the Royal Theatre, Copenhagen, to feed his own notions of how the British theatre might progress.

There was plenty of talk and plenty of ink expended for a hundred years before England gained its National Theatre. That this was not built until after his death would have been less of a surprise to Craig than to the urgent pioneers who saw a real hope of getting the foundations laid while Edward was still on the throne. Craig's reservations about institutions and his views on subsidy and commercialism tended to be erratic, but, as ever, much of what he wrote holds more than a germ of truth for the theatre of today. He would surely have been relieved that his 'advice' was taken and that an English National Theatre Company was formed and established at the Old Vic before moving to

the National Theatre complex half a mile away on the South Bank of
London's River Thames.

For the rest, his own plea for a theatre in which to work cannot be
separated from the work he wished to do in it. If the opposition offered
in his Dialogues is hardly more adequate than that offered to Socrates
in his Platonic models, it was probably a fair reflection of the commercial enthusiasm for a man whose declared aim was to offer the
tyranny of the director above all those factors which actually brought
people in at the box-office.

The Art of the Theatre was Craig's first piece of theoretical writing
of any length. Originally published by itself in 1905, it formed a natural
centre to the group of essays brought out six years later as *On the Art
of the Theatre*. Seventy years on from then it can still claim to be one of
the fundamental documents of the modern stage.

The form of a Platonic dialogue is a useful one for stating the un-
orthodox or whatever requires special pleading. It is an indication of
how revolutionary Craig's sentiments were that he had no accepted
term to describe what we now call the 'director'. Craig writes of both
'stage manager' and 'stage director'. In *Scene* he was the 'master of the
drama', though there he was speaking in broader terms. Elsewhere he
uses both *regisseur* and *metteur-en-scène*. It is perhaps worth recalling
that as few as a dozen years ago there was considerable confusion over
the difference between producer and director, until the British theatre
adopted by general agreement the distinction initially supplied by
Hollywood.

The First Dialogue is quite simply a plea for the director as overlord,
the individual who fashions a performance from author's blueprint to
finished product, and marks it with his own stamp.

It is difficult sometimes to appreciate how recent a phenomenon the
director is. Though playbills from as early as 1824 refer to pantomimes
'invented and produced by . . .' the idea that a straight play needed an
independent producer was not established until the last quarter of the
nineteenth century. Many of the functions of the modern director had
existed, of course, since organised drama began, but the task of mar-
shalling actors and scenery was comfortably accommodated at different
periods by leading actor, stage manager and even book-keeper or
prompter. That the arrival on the scene of the director coincided more
or less exactly with the first use of electric light in the theatre may be
more than coincidence. In a theatre where it was possible to create
atmosphere by a new use of directional lighting, the whole emphasis of
the stage picture underwent a change. At the same time the move to-

wards psychological motivation of character in the newer plays opened the door to interpretations of old ones in ways more far-reaching than simply adapting the leading character to the leading actor and fashionable morality. If that seems to undervalue the 'direction' of Garrick, Charles Kean or even Irving, it can hardly be denied that their productions were designed primarily to show off themselves as actors.

By the time that Craig was undertaking his earliest productions, Duke George of Saxe-Meiningen and his director, Kronek, had inspired Stanislavsky and Nemirovich-Danchenko with the ensemble work of a thoroughly rehearsed company, while Antoine and Brahm were seeking to build new kinds of stage truth. Theatres were springing up all over Europe known not because of the leading actor or house dramatist but because of their director. For the first time it became accepted at least in the independent theatres that the rehearsal process should be something more than a lines run for the minor characters.

Craig states the case for the director as supreme artist. He is able to do so principally because he was as much a designer as a director, perhaps more so. The number of occasions when he was able to exercise the total control he advocates here were strictly limited, though he often succeeded in influencing one function through another. Though he asks for the theatre of the future to be based on the freedom of the director as 'author of the spectacle', perhaps even he might have been surprised by how quickly the major theatres of the continent were to be dominated by directors whose beliefs in the priorities of the stage were to change the theatre almost overnight.

Proposals Old and New (1910)

A DIALOGUE BETWEEN A THEATRICAL MANAGER AND AN ARTIST OF THE THEATRE

Foreword
In this dialogue, although the Manager says but little, he condescends to say more than most managers. He echoes those two celebrated if slightly worn phrases that 'Art does not pay', and that 'We give the public what it demands.' He does this, we may be sure, more from habit than from any belief in their worth.

I have purposely kept the Manager from attempting to prove that what he offers in public is either original or beautiful, for I felt that my readers were tired of hearing the old lie over again. So I have kept him as quiet as

possible, unwilling that he should destroy any remaining chance of retaining esteem for his methods, or sympathy for his appalling cause. I hope in this way not to have done him any injustice.

MANAGER: That is the finest scene I ever saw. But you can't realise yon drawing upon the stage.

ARTIST: You are right: I cannot.

MANAGER: Then, if you cannot reproduce it, why do you show it to me?

ARTIST: To make an impression on you. Why ask me absurd questions?

MANAGER: Because I wish to be practical; I wish to protect my interests.

ARTIST: But you are not protecting them; you are utterly at my mercy, and seem to be trying to ruin them.

MANAGER: Really, you look at things in a strange way. Now come down to earth and tell me how we can realise yon design upon the stage.

ARTIST: We cannot; I have told you so repeatedly, but you were so quick with your questions that you would not let me tell you something which saves the situation. That design, as I have just said, is made to give you a certain impression. When I make the same scene on the stage it is sure to be quite different in form and colour, but it will create the same impression on you as this design in front of you now.

MANAGER: Two things quite different will create the same impression? Are you joking?

ARTIST: No, I am not joking; but I will do so if you insist upon it.

MANAGER: No, tell me more; explain what you mean.

ARTIST: Well, a design for a scene on paper is one thing; a scene on the stage is another. The two have no connection with each other. Each depends on a hundred different ways and means of creating the same impression. Try to adapt the one to the other and you get at best only a good translation. You do not understand? I know it; but what would you have? You ought to be content *not* to understand – *never* to understand; if you could comprehend you would have no need to consult me.

MANAGER: Well, it sounds very risky.

ARTIST: It is; terribly risky – for you. That is my point; that is the artist's everlasting point. He thinks; you risk. If you begin thinking everything is lost. Leave that to your stage manager – to me. You shall have no other risk but me. Risk me, and you stand the chance of gaining all. Avoid that risk, and you run no chance of winning anything.

MANAGER: You terrify me. I think you must be mad.

ARTIST: And you have only one thing to be careful about; you must
take care to study the difference between the different types of men
the world calls 'artists'. Sort them out, avoid the commercial fellows
and search for the 'mad' artist (I think you said mad). If you can find
one I promise you you've found a fortune. Then risk him; play him
first on the red and then on the black; throw him where you will,
he's sure to bring you luck. But my dear sir, whatever you do, pray
gamble like a gentleman; risk enormously, hazard all on this *surety*;
risk with decency, I beg; do not incessantly alter your mind – and for
heaven's sake don't apologise for your method of play!

MANAGER: Upon my word, you are an original being!

ARTIST: I am. I thought that was why you came to me. All artists are
'original' to businessmen and all businessmen are 'original' to artists;
both can truthfully be called eccentrics. This is as it should be, the
securest foundation for a successful union. The mistake is for either
of them to try and understand how the other works. Each should
remain ignorant of the other's methods, and they should unite to a
common madness called the 'concentric'. This would be very productive, very economic. Sometimes we get a man who is both artist
and businessman; Cecil Rhodes was such a man. He used the soil of
a continent as a sculptor uses a handful of clay, and from it he
fashioned United South Africa – and we shall probably learn in time
that he made something even vaster than that. Learn to risk, my
friend; and learn also that ideas are rare things, and that most artists
are packed full of ideas. Therefore the artist is the finest of all
commodities in the market.

MANAGER: But what if an idea doesn't pay?

ARTIST: An idea which doesn't pay has not yet been discovered. If
you don't know *how* to make it pay that is not a matter I can interfere
in, for if I interfere I overstep your frontiers. If you cannot make it
pay, that but reveals your ignorance of how to handle it, and you fail
at your own game – but, observe, the idea has not failed. It waits for
some one better fitted to develop it.

MANAGER: So you put the whole blame of failure on the manager or
businessman, not on the artist?

ARTIST: Yes, on the handling, and more especially so in the case of a
very original idea. With ordinary ideas it is somewhat different.
Ordinary ideas are generally rather weak, and then the only blame
which can be attached to the businessman is that he wasted too much
time and money on working a poor field. Then the whole blame lies

with the artist. The rare fields are the valuable ones, and in the realms of art the rarest field is that where the most original idea is buried. Let a shrewd businessman stake all he has on that field; with patience and determination it will yield him all he desires.

MANAGER: Yes – but to return to practical matters –

ARTIST: I had never departed from them.

MANAGER: I am speaking of this design for a scene which strikes me as quite wonderful. How are we to realise that on the stage?

ARTIST: To answer your question I must first ask you another. If we were standing on the edge of a very rich gold field and long veins of pure gold were proved to be lying buried under your very nose, and I were to ask you how to 'realise' that gold, would you not answer me that the ore was not of practical commercial value until extracted, washed, removed to the mint, and coined? In fact, changed entirely from its present entrancing condition and transformed into another, yet equally valuable, condition and form? Well, I answer you in the same way about this scene. And what is more, I advise you to work the mine from which that design came, and it will yield you all that you desire. But don't attempt the task with one pick and a shovel. Put money into it – all your money – don't be frightened. I happen to be a man with imagination, and in art that is the equivalent of a gold mine; it only needs to be properly worked. You will say I have no false modesty about myself. Certainly not, sir; the best artists from time immemorial have always known how to value their powers. Fools call it conceit, but wise men know differently.

MANAGER: Why have not businessmen done as you suggest before now?

ARTIST: They have. They did so in the fifteenth century; the Renaissance could not have happened without them. They did so in Athens: they did so in Egypt; they may do so in England and will in America. In fact they have always done so except when a wave of timidity has swept over the earth and created a panic. We are just about to emerge from such a wave; it is the psychological moment.

MANAGER: And now you expect to see everyone spending more money upon works of art?

ARTIST: Certainly I expect to see shrewd businessmen investing their money in ideas; and I expect to see these two types of man, artist and businessman, combine and place good things before the public instead of worthless things. In many instances good things are already before the public; but in the branch of public service in which we are engaged you must agree with me (knowing what you know), that the public is cheated.

MANAGER: But art doesn't pay in this branch of the service.

ARTIST: Again you make the ancient excuse. Art pays no worse, no better than anything else *if you know how to make it pay*; so I fail to see what other excuse you can make for not serving the public honestly and letting the band strike up at once.

MANAGER: Do you insinuate that I cheat the public?

ARTIST: No – I say it openly.

MANAGER: I give them what they demand.

ARTIST: Another excuse – the same one that I've heard for years. Why can't you invent some more reliable answers than '*It doesn't pay*', and '*I give the public what it demands*'? You probably think that what you are saying is true, but still that does not alter the fact that you are saying what is false.

It is false in many ways. You should know quite well that the public is so vast, is composed of so many different classes and types, its tastes varying with each type, that it is sheer lunacy to assert that there is no public for works of art. It is as much as to say that the public is incapable of appreciation. If this were so, you would have to explain how it is that the public knows the difference between a good loaf of bread and a bad one? or explain how it is that the public can discern a good day from a rainy day – how it knows a good song and a good horse from a bad song and horse? Realise that the public knows everything that is good from everything that is bad; in fact the public is as right as rain; let us hear no more criticisms of it. If you choose to criticise *a small section of the public*, that is another matter, especially if you choose that small section which grumbles at the nation's best soldiers, sailors, statesmen, judges, doctors, priests, and artists. Yet, far from criticising this section, *it is the very section you deliberately cater for in the theatre*, for those who form it are always tired after their day's grumbling and need amusement of the dullest kind. And you call that handful of the nation 'the public'. Pouff!

MANAGER: You do not convince me. I am certain that if the public wanted works of art it would create a demand for them.

ARTIST: My dear sir, you encourage me. You say the very thing I wanted you to say. 'To create a demand.' You realise that a public demand is CREATED and does not create itself. You realise that the nation entrusts certain of its officers with the different tasks of creating this, that and the other, and amongst these things is the 'creating a demand'. The public cannot speak for itself; if the whole lot speak at once no one is heard; if one man speaks he is not listened to unless he is elected as spokesman by the whole nation. Now who has the nation elected to speak for it about this matter of art? No one. Therefore until it does elect some representative, how shall we know its wishes?

MANAGER: But two hundred thousand men and women visited the Grand Theatre to see *Julius Caesar* and thereby –

ARTIST: Two hundred thousand people are not the public, and the directors of the public taste in theatrical matters are self-elected. A fine state of affairs indeed!

MANAGER: What would you propose doing to discern the tastes of the nation?

ARTIST (*looking long at him – and wondering what is the very easiest method for the poor old boy to try*): I should propose that you should try to go to the people. Send companies round England and America for the purpose of collecting votes for and against certain types of play and certain ways of producing plays. Let these companies play three plays by Shakespeare – *Hamlet, The Merchant of Venice,* and *Henry V;* a play by Sheridan and one by Ibsen; a play by Goldsmith and one by Goldoni; a play by Molière and a modern French problem play; a play by Shaw, one by Strindberg, one by Synge and one by Yeats, and one Pantomime or Dumb-show drama. Let these plays be produced very carefully by the different stage managers keen for the competition. Let this company call at every centre in England and America, and afterwards at several of the smaller towns, and let the people record their votes for and against the different pieces. Of course, the question at issue will have to be laid clearly before them, and their serious consideration of the pieces requested.

The journals all over England and America would take the matter up and would help to make this question clear. The best journals would point out to their readers that the question was one of those affecting the national welfare, and a difficult one to answer, and would help the people to see the difference between a healthy and an unhealthy drama; between a romantic or poetic treatment and a drab and realistic treatment. The excitement created by this tour of the States would in all probability create a new and serious interest in the theatre, and the whole country would at last be glad to take up the matter of State theatres.

Such a plan as I have sketched out roughly for you is capable of development, and is just the kind of thing that would encourage the theatre. It would cost money, but it would bring in money, and the direct advantages to be derived from such a step are as obvious as they are enormous. Here then is an opportunity for a businessman of ability to make his mark. After this test you will probably be surprised to find that the public has all along been opposed to the rubbish which it is forced to accept at the theatre in place of good stuff.

MANAGER: And what do you think the public wishes?

ARTIST: All that is good. It wants good statesmen and good fighters in an emergency, and it gets them. It wants good amusements and good art. The first it sometimes gets; the second is withheld from it. The cinemas, the vaudevilles, and the circuses provide admirable amusement. The theatre should provide for its art. Popular art? Certainly popular art. When certain sections of the public wish for relaxation they find it in the music hall. Excellent! But when another section of the public wants something better than leather, it looks for it and can't find it, and is disappointed. Think how invigorating Shakespeare could be made to that enormous section of the public who work with their brains all day! Think of the doctors, priests, writers, painters, musicians, architects, city men, engineers, army and navy men, politicians, secretaries, editors, journalists, and other social men and women to whom a vigorous living theatre might prove *refreshing*, and who are today obliged to avoid the place because it is wearisome – a bore.

It is utterly impossible to believe that the failure of the theatre today is due to a low standard of public taste. Public taste was never better than it is going to be tomorrow. You might test the statement by the method I have suggested, and you will be doing a great thing for the nation, or by any method except the mad methodless way you set about it, but anyhow, whatever way you set about it, get up early, if you want to be in time.

from *Rearrangements* (1915)

... we find that the body of the modern theatre is composed of strangely contradictory elements; of the organic and the inorganic hopelessly clinging together.

Regard for a moment this bunch of confusion; and first regard that side where all the stage conventions and inventions are clustered.

We find:

1. On the poet's part, an unnatural mode of speech – verse or prose.

2. On the actor's part, a natural, even colloquial mode of utterance.
3. Scenes imitating nature in paint and canvas.
4. Actors of flesh and blood.
5. Movements half natural, half artificial.
6. Light always failing in an attempt to simulate Nature's light.
7. The faces painted and disguised.
8. The facial expression always attempting to come through the paint and disguise.

Thus in 1, 2, 4 and 8 – the words, actors, their speech and facial expression are organic.

3 and 7 – the scenes and the disguised faces are inorganic.

5 and 6 – the light and movement are half one thing and half the other.

It is with this material that the modern theatre fatuously believes it can fashion a work of art. And it is against this material that the nature of all art rebels and prevails.

Let us rearrange and change parts of this conglomeration and then see whether things are not more of a piece. And against those items which we rearrange or change we will place a sign (§), so that it will be seen at a glance.

1. The poet's work to be as it is – an unnatural mode of speech, or verse.
§2. The actor's work to be an unnatural mode of delivery.
§3. The scene to be a non-natural invention, timeless, and of no locality.
§4. Actors to be disguised beyond recognition, like the marionette.
§5. Movements conventionalised according to some system.
§6. Light frankly non-natural, disposed so as to illumine scene and actors.
§7. Masks.
§8. Expression to be dependent on the masks and the conventional movements, both of which are dependent on the skill of the actor.

Now we find that without having to eliminate any one of the eight factors, we have been able to harmonise their conflicting purposes by altering some of them.

But let us once again rearrange the parts so that they harmonise in another key.

§1. The poet's work to be written in a colloquial mode of speech, natural – as improvisation is.

2. The actor's delivery to be colloquial.

§3. The scene to be a facsimile or photographic reproduction of nature, even to the use of real trees, real earth, bricks, etc.

4. The actors in no ways disguised, but selected according to their likeness to the part which is to be acted.

5. Movements as natural as the speech.

6. The light of day or night.

7. The faces of the actors paintless.

8. The expression as natural as the movements and speech.

Now either of these two arrangements is logical in itself, even as it would be logical to place a real chrysanthemum in a real glass vase with real water in it, or an imitation flower in a papier-maché vase painted to look as though it held water.

In short, to mix the real and the unreal, the genuine and the sham – *when you are not forced to do so* – is at all times, whether in life or in art, an error, a misconception of the nature of all things, a parody of purpose.

The next question therefore seems to be, which is the best of the two logical rearrangements?

'Best' is often a matter of opinion, and always so where the decision is unhampered by tradition. Tradition also is fallible, yet where we benefit greatly by following a tradition, should we not do unwisely to depart from it?

Thus, I hardly think that in the case of ship-building we should break through the old tradition of putting a keel to our ships, nor even skirt round the tradition by making the keels of leather. Yet doubtless some who have an exaggerated regard for their own opinion in face of expert opinion will stick to it that leather keels are best when the other parts of a ship are made of iron and steel – for 'there is nothing like leather'.

Therefore I cannot help feeling that since, for ages and not merely centuries, all art experts – that is to say, artists and art theorists too – have decided that, no matter what the work is to be, if it is to be called an art work it must be made solely from *inorganic* material, the first rearrangement that I have suggested is *nearer* the desired state than is the second; not perfect, but at least nearer.

I am aware that in the first rearrangement there are some suggestions which will strike you as uncommon. Let me assure you that they are really not all new, if rather unfamiliar to us. If they *appear* strange it is because they have been for a long time disregarded and are in disuse.

But we find that even in poetry, in music, and in architecture an old rhythm or scale which has been long forgotten is found agreeable by the artist who, when he employs it, startles his audience a little. They think it is his invention, unaware that it has a tradition of centuries to commend its use.

I would propose, therefore, that we familiarise ourselves and our assistants with these seemingly new suggestions until we realise their *value*; and that where, by the addition and application of one or more of these suggestions we can increase the value of the whole Art of the Theatre, we should not be held up by an over-sensitive lack of confidence in our power to apply them, or by lack of faith in the power of the spectators to accept them.

This is one method of advancing our institution to a position which may influence the distinguished traducers of our work to consider their verdict that the Art of the Theatre is an *inferior* art.

Theatrical Reform (1910)

There is far too much haste about all this reform, far too much haste. Nearly everyone concerned in it seems to be frightened of time, and in this haste the good energy is wasted.

Each day, week and month we read energetic statements made, or hasty conclusions formed by enthusiasts.

Those enthusiasts should pull up, and discipline themselves a little. Instead of leaping quickly to conclusions they should begin at the beginning and search for the truth. That would bring them to the end of their lives in a more contented frame of mind than they promise to reach it in at present.

The enthusiasts are the only people who count, but the sum reaches a very low figure when they let their enthusiasm carry them away.

For example, an enthusiast for the theatre has only to see one performance given in the open air with a background of trees, let us say by some 'forest players', to believe that the solution of the riddle of the theatre lies in taking the theatre into the open air.

Another enthusiast believes that the whole thing is to be solved when the dance is thoroughly understood.

The third believes that it is all a matter of the scenery.

A fourth is sure that it is a question of artificial lighting.

A fifth is positive that it has something to do with socialism, and that if plays dealing with the labour movement are put before the audience the whole theatre will revive.

The sixth enthusiast thinks the reproduction of actual life on the stage is the secret.

The seventh is convinced that it is something to do with the community, and that a communal theatre would solve the riddle.

An eighth thinks instead that the reproduction of the ancient drama, Greek or Elizabethan, in theatres most like to those in which they originated, would solve the riddle.

The ninth enthusiast (for the impresarios are enthusiasts in their own way) thinks that the whole thing is a question of dollars.

And so, as I have said, day after day these voices are heard making these announcements with all the finality of the inexpert.

Alas, these gentlemen in their haste are of assistance to but one set of people only; to those who wish to make money out of the theatre.

For the clever businessman can take any one reform, and successfully tackle it, and turn it into a good paying concern, because when the show takes place the reform will not be noticed, but only a certain sense of novelty will be felt. That is just what he wants.

The open-air enthusiasts are merely playing into the hands of the impresarios who come along with, say, a *Joan of Arc* produced with a quantity of French or German help, and makes fifty per cent for himself, and fifty per cent to the score of vulgarity. A certain club in California is doing exactly the same. And those enthusiasts, because they get 'near to nature', think that they are getting near to the soul of the folk, and expect some miraculous folk-drama to result from the coquetting of the theatre and its painted face and gaudy trappings with the brambles and the redwood trees.

In the same way some enthusiasts in Russia, in Germany, in Denmark, in Switzerland, in France and in England, who are studying the theory of Delsarte and making their limbs nice and supple, and producing dances as sweet as the chocolates in the celebrated box, are but playing into the hands of the impresario. They are certainly doing nothing to aid in the rebirth of the theatre.

Signor Fortunio, Herr Littmanbachstein with their elaborate lighting effects, the young Munich and London artists with their scenic effects, the Futurists of yesterday afternoon, are all serving the cause of the businessman.

The Socialist theatre reformer with his ponderous labour plays has for some time been annexed by businessmen and we have their word for it that it is paying.

The reformer with realistic tendencies who reproduces an actual room, actual manners and other actual sights and sounds, will of course be a very useful if rather expensive man to rake in the pounds, shillings and pence for Monsieur Impresario.

As I have said before, each of these reformers, taken separately, can be of value to the businessman. Taken together only can they crush him. They can only crush him when they combine, and on the day that they do combine I would not give two pins for the cleverest businessman on the face of the earth. On that day the theatre will begin to pull itself together.

Certainly the question of the open air must come to be considered, but it must not be considered enthusiastically, but coolly, and from many different points of view before anything valuable can be done.

The thing in itself, the idea in itself, creates enthusiasm in whoever thinks about it, but we must not rush into the open air and begin to wave our arms, and quote Shakespeare, and think we have achieved something by doing so.

This is abominable and utterly unworthy of the good fellows who carry on in that way. As I have said, it shows haste. They are frightened of time. They feel they are going to be left behind. If they did not feel this they would take a little longer to consider the question: 'How to act in the open air, and what is the difference between such acting and that destined for a roofed theatre?' And this question leads up to so many other questions that very few persons are able to answer them today, and certainly not in a hurry.

So it is with the dance. What is its actual relationship to the theatre, and, considering our first question, its relation to the theatre of the open air in distinction to the roofed-in theatre? No one can hastily don a few Egyptian clothes, and, relying upon personality, come before the world and claim to have discovered a new theatre in a *pas seul*. Dance may or may not have its place in the Art of the Theatre; to judge from the elect who choose to copy Isadora Duncan's *manner* instead of acknowledging her magic, and refraining once and for ever, most probably it has not; but this cannot be decided in a hurry.

With painted scenery, and with the lighting of this modern scene the same judgement has to be passed. You may not claim to have discoverd the new Art of the Theatre on the score that you have designed and lighted some original scenes.

Again, because you have dealt with a few Socialistic questions of the day in some plays you must not believe that you have created a new drama.

Reform may or may not come through reforming theatre construction, dance, scene, lighting, motif of plays, the box-office and acting; but such reform can only be at all valuable after the reformers become

united in friendship, and are in closer communion, and their followers
following, instead of barking in the wings.

I hope that before long these enthusiasts who are at present divided
will unite, and prove again in the history of the theatre the power of
real and disinterested enthusiasm, coupled with sound judgement – and
that they will recognise that *service* is the very nearest thing to *magic*.

from *A Production* (1930)

All things will be possible in London as soon as you re-establish a solid
base of moral courage in the theatres. As it is, nothing is possible,
because those who are to be heard saying, 'Damn it – Craig's work is
what we want' are the very fellows who wilt at the very first
objection . . .

Johannes Poulsen has moral courage and he stood firmly to me: I do
not know of one English theatre man who has done so for over three
days. The first breath of wind – the first adverse opinion – the first
reason against my work or against me – or against the way my dog lifts
his leg against lamp-posts, sweeps away the firm resolve of the English
theatre men who have professed their intention of seeing the thing
through . . . 'by God, sir' . . .

But suppose any one such ally should appear in London, he might
not quite realise that while moral courage is the first necessary asset,
there are still other things necessary before any serious and lasting good
can be achieved to the benefit of the British theatre. A glance at the
Copenhagen theatre shows what is required:

1. One man of moral courage.
2. A theatre financially sound.
3. A permanent company of actors, of singers, of dancers, *trained
   from childhood*.
4. A discipline founded upon courtesy, preserved by good rules and a
   proper realisation of *esprit de corps*.
5. The best technical equipment in Europe.
6. A permanent staff of technicians with years of training behind
   them.
7. A permanent staff of administrators and their assistants.
8. A permanent staff of scenic and costume artists and their assistants.
9. A permanent staff of stage-carpenters, scene-shifters, and every
   kind of theatre workman and workwoman.

10. A school for the *daily* training of actors, singers, dancers, scenic artists, costumiers, and others.
11. *Not* a National Theatre, though the Copenhagen theatre is that.
12. A private theatre, established independently by men who care to see the British theatre the best in Europe and determine to make it and keep it so.
13. No outside interference.
14. King and country with you.

We could have had today one of the finest theatres in the world if, twenty-five years ago, at the death of Irving, we had not all raised a howl saying 'what can follow after this?'. . . . it is (I had better say it since nobody else will) one of the minor jokes of the age that my services have been dispensed with. Let no one suppose that I imagine myself to be a very great genius with astounding gifts – but I am a useful stage director, possibly one of the most useful that England has produced in the last twenty-five years.

Isn't it comic? For I have been unemployed in England for twenty-five years.

from *An International Symposium* (1909)

QUESTION: Do you believe a national theatre, directed by a committee, is advantageous to the development of our artists?

GORDON CRAIG: . . . I do not. A committee is often less capable of keeping its temper than an individual. And the theatre is trying to the temper as it was in 400 B.C. in Greece, and in 400 A.D. in Rome, and in the Middle Ages in Italy. Apollo and Dionysus are still at war in the theatre. Pulcinello still fights Roscius and the minstrel squabbles with both; whilst the new actor, the socially immaculate one, threatens to filch with hypocritical hands the very soul of the theatre and put it in his pocket. It is well he should not be a social anarchist, but to have accidentally washed away his talent with his roguery and vagabondage was not clever of him.

To me there seems but one way to save the theatre from itself; it is to remove the art out of the theatre; to transfer it to a place of safety for a certain period; to a university or to a church, and there to await developments.

QUESTION: Do you think greater advantage would accrue to the State if it supported the independent efforts of individual artists of great talent, rather than a collective and less talented body of artists under the control of a committee?

GORDON CRAIG: The State, like everything else, has itself to support. It rests with itself to decide whether a noble and non-commercial theatre is more beneficial to its health than a degraded and money-making theatre; and the difficult task it sets itself is to discern the difference between a noble theatre and a claptrap theatre. The latter class of theatre can be observed any day from the comfortable seat of a hansom cab if the driver is directed to go down Shaftesbury Avenue, the Haymarket, then down to St James' Palace, back through Pall Mall into St Martin's Lane and then down the Strand. The non-commercial theatre must be imagined. This is not so difficult . . . with practice, and when once it has been imagined by the artist the State has the power to assist in the realisation of the dream.

Theatre and English Theatre (1924)

These are not one and the same thing.

The theatre is a world thing: the theatre of England is a local thing. In the world theatre the theatre of England has a place, but not the first place. Its place is near the French theatre. The French theatre will not protest when we remind it that Shakespeare (though exiled by us) is still a member of our theatre, and a name we use to conjure with.

While the Russian, German and Italian theatres cannot show a star of such magnitude and brilliance as Shakespeare or Molière, they are today taking more forward positions than those to which the French and English manipulators are happy to see their two theatres relegated.

The Russians, Germans and Italians use the best brains of their theatres.

The American theatre is awake to possibilities.

The English theatre concerns us most. We would like to see it in a more leading position.

The English theatre is hide-bound. It continues to allow the same old underhand manipulators of the lasty forty years to muddle things. Its critics, if old, mutter the same contented platitudes; if young, a five years course of the underhand professionalism soon brings them to toe the line and mumble what they are told to mumble.

If this be good enough for you, it is not good enough for us. But how get along with things, . . . how get things better . . . how establish a theatre that is worth while?

By establishing a National Theatre? That might prove to be merely a waste of public money, for some of those interested in seeing it established are too self-interested. We are not ready for a National Theatre, for we have nothing to put into it. Names are nothing. Shakespeare is a name and we have rendered it a valueless one today, for we cannot do justice to one of his works; at best we can but vamp happily, or sentimentally, through one or two. By saying this we would not undervalue the work of the Old Vic whose members we believe to be an honest group of workers. The Old Vic may do good work; it is spoken of as one of the best companies at present in harness; but it is not greatly gifted enough, not powerful enough, to restore to Shakespeare his old values. Which are immense.

Honest men working without thought of self, we must have; but we must also have an honest man of brains and imagination as their leader.

Not until England chooses to drive away the hundreds of petty somebodies, ceases straining an ear to the mumbling of certain critics, those poseurs who have kept our theatre under for these last twenty years, not till then will there be room for the better workers. Until England clears out the underhand professional 'manipulators' and invites the new men in, the English theatre will be forced into the background by other European theatres.

Until all the artists, and the whole art of the theatre, be reinstated in the English theatre, and placed under one leader, the old critics may mumble in good prose and the young critics may cry out for mild reforms; . . . all is useless. The English theatre will remain in the place it now fills with such unnecessary distinction, – a back seat.

from *The Art of the Theatre. The Second Dialogue* (1910)

PLAYGOER: Well, we are going to have a National Theatre in England.
STAGE DIRECTOR: Not at all. We are going to have a Society Theatre. That in my opinion is very much what the new theatre in America is – a society theatre. Now nobody wants a society theatre, least of all the ladies and gentlemen who are obliged to go and sit in their boxes and stalls while they are bored to death by the dull performances which take place on the stage. Such society theatres bore and impoverish every city of Europe. There is the Opéra in Paris, the Schauspielhaus in Berlin, in Munich, in Vienna. They are not national theatres in the real sense of the word. The men who will make a national theatre in England are the same kind of men as those who have made this theatre in Russia. If they are to be expensive they must not be a bore, these theatres. The proposed 'national' theatre for London is national in name only. It has no programme, and yet it asks for subscriptions on the strength of one. The committee may

force subscriptions, but no amount of forcing can raise the wits – and it is wits and taste that we want in our theatre. Now the Russians commence founding their national theatre by first founding an artistic theatre and testing its honesty of purpose for ten years. Which of these strikes you as the better method of obtaining a finely organised national theatre – the English or the Russian? Which is the most economic, the most regular? Which seems to you the *rightest*? In short, if you had a theatre which method would you yourself employ?

PLAYGOER: The Russian method – if I had the type of men and the same point of view.

from *Scene* (1923)

And it should be the pleasure of all workers in the dramatic art to see to it that nothing is out of place . . . and no one out of place.

It should be the pleasure and duty of them all to put the drama in order again, and the Master of the Drama in his place – at the head of all.

And who is this Master, and what his duties?

He is the best man.

Now the best man at drama must be the best man at theatres and at playing with theatricals.

At one period he is *Molière*, the actor–writer. At another time *Sophocles*, dancer–actor–writer. At a third time *Andreini*, actor only. At a fourth time *Shakespeare*, actor–writer. In each period you see the best man was actor. They say that Molière was not a good actor; – what they mean I do not know: that Shakespeare was not a great actor, acted only minor parts: . . . maybe. These two were in a theatre – each in ONE theatre only: . . . did not pop from one to another company; gave time and nature a chance to develop – grew like plants – flowered – bore fruit . . .

All these men thought in terms of the stage – lived theatre – brought man, mountains, passions, sun, light, dreams, ghosts, into the theatre: not only by means of words – by any means they could contrive – and to the end of time this will be so and may be so.

And should it happen some day that one who has the actor's talent should be architect (as was Albergati in 1480 and Ariosti in 1530), he may combine his two talents towards creating drama, and in his own way – yes, even breaking little traditions. It is permitted.

Should he be actor or painter and writer, he too may use these three talents to create drama . . . and a fourth if he possess it. But no one who is not primarily actor can quite hope to create drama.

This is what I mean when I speak of the Master of Drama being a man of the theatre.

Another can write plays – these can be often excellent, as *She Stoops to Conquer* is excellent, or as *On ne badine pas avec l'amour*; but they *have* not the genuine touch of the true-bred dramatist.

Never would I hold that a painter or a writer can be true dramatist – using their powers over design and over words – and these alone. Never have I held so. Always have I been misrepresented as holding these views.

I have heard even one great play-writer publicly saying that I am a painter . . . and that my scenes are all I am thinking of.

I have made scenes – this is because I see a need, – and possess a talent, for making the place or scene in which drama has to move.

But I have been actor – and I am primarily that: I am able to write a little. I consider no time lost which is spent towards qualifying as a master (though maybe only a little master) of the theatre – and thus, maybe, of drama. So much as apology for my shortcomings.

And here we will go on to consider what are the duties of a Master of the Drama and Theatre.

They are today, to recognise that the theatre as work-place – its stage, scene, actors, and other assistants, is an unwieldy, untidy, and unpractical affair at best, and (I think) to set to work first to simplify it, and then re-elaborate it, and both with the utmost caution.

To simplify an affair of this kind time is necessary. It cannot be done in a month – nor in ten months; maybe not even in ten years.

And to simplify it you must first come to know it so well that as you eliminate you do not reject an essential part of the machine. To simplify the stage has been the work I have devoted myself to for the last twenty-five years.

I think I have done what I set out to do.

Whether there remains time for me to do what further I had in view remains to be seen.

Now, what I simplified was not merely bits of scenery, and lighting effects, rags of costume and incidental music.

I simplified the possibilities of drama.

No scene that I worked at was worked at for its own sake. I thought solely of the movement of the drama . . . of the actors . . . of the dramatic moments . . . those long, slow movements and those 'flashes of lightning' (Coleridge). I saw as I progressed that things can, and there-fore should, play their parts as well as people: that they combine with the actor and plead for the actor to use them, as the chairs in Molière's plays testify. Not merely are they three or four dead chairs which he placed on the centre of the stage. Yet writers call on us to regard the emptiness of his stage – merely three chairs, they say. Are they mad, these men? Don't they know how Molière made these chairs act – how they are *alive*, and working in combination with the actors?

The chairs and tables in modern plays of which the great Italian actress complains are dead, – there may be six more or sixteen more, or six less; all is as it was . . . dead scene . . . a curse to actors and acting.

A so-called 'real' room is what we present on a stage today, . . . real and yet quite dead – expressionless – unable to act.

Molière's chairs, tables properties of all kinds, were few; he had learned from Italy that they had to be few to be heard – and each of them had to speak at the right moment.

Shakespeare's properties could speak too – although Cromwell and his puritans tore out their tongues and almost dehumanised the whole Shakespearian drama for us.

The tradition once lost, it has never quite recovered its original force.

So, then, to create a simplified stage is the first duty of a master of the drama.

Not by rejecting electricity because of its defects: not by returning to tallow candles: not by returning to masks: by *avoidance* of nothing, by *returning* to nothing – but by this process . . .

By reviewing all the theatrical things known of or once known of as serviceable to the stage, . . . testing them in private, and rejecting those which seem hollow and useless, and retaining all those which stand the test.

What test? – the test whether or no they are capable of expression. That and little else. We must ask ourselves –

Does a wax candle serve us to express the rising sun? – If yes, then use it. Does it not serve? – then reject it. But test it first – pooh-pooh nothing till you've tested it. Does a mask serve us to express such and such a human emotion? If it does, use it; – if not, away with it. Does chanting serve any purpose? – if so, what purpose? – is it of value? – then retain chanting: if none, away with it. Does this or that system of gesture serve? – preserve it – or be done with it. Can actors be taught? – to what extent? Which form of stage is the right one for such and such a play – which next best, which least good. Choose the best. Does it not exist? Then build one. Whatever the answers, abide by them. These and a hundred other notions – hopes – fears – have all to be tested to simplify that machine known as the theatre. This will prove very expensive you may fancy. Fancy is not to be relied on, fact is more sure and fact shows us that to avoid testing everything is the most expensive method of all.

The Art of the Theatre. The First Dialogue (1905)

An expert and a playgoer are conversing.

STAGE DIRECTOR: You have now been over the theatre with me, and have seen its general construction, together with the stage, the machinery for manipulating the scenes, the apparatus for lighting, and the hundred other things, and have also heard what I have had to say of the theatre as a machine; let us rest here in the auditorium, and talk a while of the theatre and of its art. Tell me, do you know what is the Art of the Theatre?

PLAYGOER: To me it seems that acting is the Art of the Theatre.

STAGE DIRECTOR: Is a part, then, equal to a whole?

PLAYGOER: No, of course not. Do you, then, mean that the play is the Art of the Theatre?

STAGE DIRECTOR: A play is a work of literature, is it not? Tell me, then, how one art can possibly be another?

PLAYGOER: Well, then, if you tell me that the Art of the Theatre is neither the acting nor the play, then I must come to the conclusion that it is the scenery and the dancing. Yet I cannot think you will tell me this is so.

STAGE DIRECTOR: No; the Art of the Theatre is neither acting nor the play, it is not scene nor dance, but it consists of all the elements of which these things are composed: action, which is the very spirit of acting; words, which are the body of the play; line and colour, which are the very heart of the scene; rhythm, which is the very essence of dance.

PLAYGOER: Action, words, line, colour, rhythm! And which of these is all-important to the art?

STAGE DIRECTOR: One is no more important than the other, no more than one colour is more important to a painter than another, or one note more important than another to a musician. In one respect, perhaps, action is the most valuable part. Action bears the same relation to the Art of the Theatre as drawing does to painting, and melody does to music. The Art of the Theatre has sprung from action – movement – dance.

PLAYGOER: I always was led to suppose that it had sprung from speech, and that the poet was the father of the theatre.

STAGE DIRECTOR: This is the common belief, but consider it for a moment. The poet's imagination finds voice in words, beautifully chosen; he then either recites or sings these words to us, and all is done. That poetry, sung or recited, is for our ears, and, through them, for our imagination. It will not help the matter if the poet shall add gesture to his recitation or to his song; in fact, it will spoil all.

PLAYGOER: Yes, that is clear to me. I quite understand that the addition of gesture to a perfect lyric poem can but produce an inharmonious result. But would you apply the same argument to dramatic poetry?

STAGE DIRECTOR: Certainly I would. Remember I speak of a dramatic poem, not of a drama. The two things are separate things. A dramatic poem is to be read. A drama is not to be read, but to be seen upon the stage. Therefore gesture is a necessity to a drama, and it is useless to a dramatic poem. It is absurd to talk of these two things, gesture and poetry, as having anything to do with one another. And now, just as you must not confound the dramatic peom with the drama, neither must you confound the dramatic poet with the dramatist. The first writes for the reader, or listener, the second writes for the audience of a theatre. Do you know who was the father of the dramatist?

PLAYGOER: No, I do not know, but I suppose he was the dramatic poet.

STAGE DIRECTOR: You are wrong. The father of the dramatist was the dancer. And now tell me from what material the dramatist made his first piece?

PLAYGOER: I suppose he used words in the same way as the lyric poet.

STAGE DIRECTOR: Again you are wrong, and that is what every one else supposes who has not learnt the nature of dramatic art. No; the dramatist made his first piece by using action, words, line, colour, and rhythm, and making his appeal to our eyes and ears by a dexterous use of these five factors.

PLAYGOER: And what is the difference between this work of the first dramatists and that of the modern dramatists?

STAGE DIRECTOR: The first dramatists were children of the theatre. The modern dramatists are not. The first dramatist understood what the modern dramatist does not yet understand. He knew that when he and his fellows appeared in front of them the audience would be more eager to *see* what he would *do* than to *hear* what he might say. He knew that the eye is more swiftly and powerfully appealed to

than any other sense; that it is without question the keenest sense of
the body of man. The first thing which he encountered on appearing
before them was many pairs of eyes, eager and hungry. Even the
men and women sitting so far from him that they would not always
be able to hear what he might say, seemed quite close to him by
reason of the piercing keenness of their questioning eyes. To these,
and all, he spoke either in poetry or prose, but always in action: in
poetic action which is dance, or in prose action which is gesture.

PLAYGOER: I am very interested, go on, go on.

STAGE DIRECTOR: No – rather let us pull up and examine our ground.
I have said that the first dramatist was the dancer's son, that is to
say, the child of the theatre, not the child of the poet. And I have
just said that the modern dramatic poet is the child of the poet, and
knows only how to reach the ears of his listeners, nothing else. And
yet in spite of this does not the modern audience still go to the
theatre as of old to see things, and not to hear things? Indeed, modern
audiences insist on looking and having their eyes satisfied in spite of
the call from the poet that they shall use their ears only And now do
not misunderstand me. I am not saying or hinting that the poet is a
bad writer of plays, or that he has a bad influence upon the theatre.
I only wish you to understand that the poet is not of the theatre, has
never come from the theatre, and cannot be of the theatre, and that
only the dramatist among writers has any birth-claim to the theatre –
and that a very slight one. But to continue. My point is this, that the
people still flock to *see*, not to hear, plays. But what does that prove?
Only that the audiences have not altered. They are there with their
thousand pairs of eyes, just the same as of old. And this is all the
more extraordinary because the playwrights and the plays have
altered. No longer is a play a balance of actions, words, dance, and
scene, but it is either all words or all scene. Shakespeare's plays, for
instance, are a very different thing to the less modern miracle and
mystery plays, which were made entirely for the theatre. *Hamlet* has
not the nature of a stage representation. *Hamlet* and the other plays
of Shakespeare have so vast and so complete a form when read, that
they can but lose heavily when presented to us after having undergone
stage treatment. That they were acted in Shakespeare's day proves
nothing. I will tell you, on the other hand, what at that period was
made for the theatre – the Masques – the Pageants – these were light
and beautiful examples of the Art of the Theatre. Had the plays been
made to be seen, we should find them incomplete when we read them.
Now, no one will say that they find *Hamlet* dull or incomplete when

they read it, yet there are many who will feel sorry after witnessing a performance of the play, saying, 'No, that is not Shakespeare's *Hamlet*.' When no further addition can be made so as to better a work of art, it can be spoken of as 'finished' – it is complete. *Hamlet* was finished – was complete – when Shakespeare wrote the last word of his blank verse, and for us to add to it by gesture, scene, costume, or dance, is to hint that it is incomplete and needs these additions.

PLAYGOER: Then do you mean to say *Hamlet* should never be performed?

STAGE DIRECTOR: To what purpose would it be if I replied 'Yes'? *Hamlet* will go on being performed for some time yet, and the duty of the interpreters is to put their best work at its service. But, as I have said, the theatre must not forever rely upon having a play to perform, but must in time perform pieces of its own art.

PLAYGOER: And a piece for the theatre, is that, then, incomplete when printed in a book or recited?

STAGE DIRECTOR: Yes – and incomplete anywhere except on the boards of a theatre. It must needs be unsatisfying, artless, when read or merely heard, because it is incomplete without its action, its colour, its line and its rhythm in movement and in scene.

PLAYGOER: This interests me, but it dazzles me at the same time.

STAGE DIRECTOR: Is that, perhaps, because it is a little new? Tell me what it is especially that dazzles you.

PLAYGOER: Well, first of all, the fact that I have never stopped to consider of what the art of the theatre consisted – to many of us it is just an amusement.

STAGE DIRECTOR: And to you?

PLAYGOER: Oh, to me it has always been a fascination, half amusement and half intellectual exercise. The show has always amused me; the playing of the players has often instructed me.

STAGE DIRECTOR: In fact, a sort of incomplete satisfaction. That is the natural result of seeing and hearing something imperfect.

PLAYGOER: But I have seen some few plays which seemed to satisfy me.

STAGE DIRECTOR: If you have been entirely satisfied by something obviously mediocre, may it not be that you were searching for something less than mediocre, and you found that which was just a little better than you expected? Some people go to the theatre, nowadays, expecting to be bored. This is natural, for they have been taught to look for tiresome things. When you tell me you have been satisfied at a modern theatre, you prove that it is not only the art which has degnerated, but that a proportion of the audience has degenerated also. But do not let this depress you. I once knew a man whose life was so occupied, he never heard music other than that of the street organ. It was to him the ideal of what music should be. Still, as you know, there is better music in the world – in fact, barrel-organ music is very bad music; and if you were for once to see an actual piece of theatrical art, you would never again tolerate what is today being thrust upon you in place of theatrical art. The reason why you are not given a work of art on the stage is not because the public does not want it, not because there are not excellent craftsmen in the theatre who could prepare it for you, but because the theatre lacks the artist – the artist of the theatre, mind you, not the painter, poet, musician. The many excellent craftsmen whom I have mentioned are, all of them, more or less helpless to change the situation. They are forced to supply what the managers of the theatre demand, but they do so most willingly. The advent of the artist in the theatre world will change all this. He will slowly but surely gather around him these better craftsmen of whom I speak, and together they will give new life to the art of the theatre.

PLAYGOER: But for the others?

STAGE DIRECTOR: The others? The modern theatre is full of these others, these untrained and untalented craftsmen. But I will say one thing for them. I believe they are unconscious of their inability. It is not ignorance on their part, it is innocence. Yet if these same men once realised that they were craftsmen, and would train as such – I do not speak only of the stage-carpenters, electricians, wigmakers, costumiers, scene-painters, and actors (indeed, these are in many ways the best and most willing craftsmen) – I speak chiefly of the stage director. If the stage director was to technically train himself for his task of interpreting the plays of the dramatist – in time, and by a gradual development he would again recover the ground lost to the theatre, and finally would restore the Art of the Theatre to its home by means of his own creative genius.

PLAYGOER: Then you place the stage director before the actors?

STAGE DIRECTOR: Yes; the relation of the stage director to the actor is precisely the same as that of the conductor to his orchestra, or of the publisher to his printer.

PLAYGOER: And you consider that the stage director is a craftsman and not an artist?

STAGE DIRECTOR: When he interprets the plays of the dramatist by means of his actors, his scene-painters, and his other craftsmen, then he is a craftsman – a master craftsman; when he will have mastered the uses of actions, words, line, colour, and rhythm, then he may become an artist. Then we shall no longer need the assistance of the playwright – for our art will then be self-reliant.

PLAYGOER: Is your belief in a Renaissance of the art based on your belief in the Renaissance of the stage director?

STAGE DIRECTOR: Yes, certainly, most certainly. Did you for an instant think that I have a contempt for the stage director? Rather have I a contempt for any man who fails in the whole duty of the stage director.

PLAYGOER: What are his duties?

STAGE DIRECTOR: What is his craft? I will tell you. His work as interpreter of the play of the dramatist is something like this: he takes the copy of the play from the hands of the dramatist and promises faithfully to interpret it as indicated in the text (remember I am speaking only of the very best of stage directors). He then reads the play, and during the first reading the entire colour, tone, movement, and rhythm that the work must assume comes clearly before him. As for the stage directions, descriptions of the scenes, etc., with which the author may interlard his copy, these are not to be considered by him, for if he is master of his craft he can learn nothing from them.

PLAYGOER: I do not quite understand you. Do you mean that when a playwright has taken the trouble to describe the scene in which his men and women are to move and talk, that the stage director is to take no notice of such directions – in fact, to disregard them?

STAGE DIRECTOR: It makes no difference whether he regards or disregards them. What he must see to is that he makes his action and scene match the verse or the prose, the beauty of it, the sense of it. Whatever picture the dramatist may wish us to know of, he will describe his scene during the progress of the conversation between the characters. Take, for instance, the first scene in *Hamlet*. It begins:

BERNARDO: Who's there?
FRANCISCO: Nay, answer me; stand and unfold yourself.
BERNARDO: Long live the king!
FRANCISCO: Bernardo?
BERNARDO: He.
FRANCISCO: You come most carefully upon your hour.
BERNARDO: 'Tis now struck twelve; get thee to bed, Francisco.
FRANCISCO: For this relief much thanks, 'tis bitter cold,
    And I am sick at heart.
BERNARDO: Have you had quiet guard?

FRANCISCO: Not a mouse stirring.
BERNARDO: Well good night.
    If you do meet Horatio and Marcellus,
    The rivals of my watch, bid them make haste.

That is enough to guide the stage director. He gathers from it that it
is twelve o'clock at night, that it is in the open air, that the guard of
some castle is being changed, that it is very cold, very quiet, and very
dark. Any additional 'stage directions' by the dramatist are triviali-
ties.

PLAYGOER: Then you do not think that an author should write any
    stage directions whatever, and you seem to consider it an offence on
    his part if he does so?

STAGE DIRECTOR: Well, is it not an offence to the men of the theatre?

PLAYGOER: In what way?

STAGE DIRECTOR: First tell me the greatest offence an actor can give
    to a dramatist.

PLAYGOER: To play his part badly?

STAGE DIRECTOR: No, that may merely prove the actor to be a bad
    craftsman.

PLAYGOER: Tell me, then.

STAGE DIRECTOR: The greatest offence an actor can give to a dram-
    atist is to cut out words or lines in his play, or to insert what is
    known as a 'gag'. It is an offence to poach on what is the sole property
    of the playwright. It is not usual to 'gag' in Shakespeare, and when it
    is done it does not go uncensured.

PLAYGOER: But what has this to do with the stage directions of the
    playwright, and in what way does the playwright offend the theatre
    when he dictates his stage directions?

STAGE DIRECTOR: He offends in that he poaches on their preserves.
    If to gag or cut the poet's lines is an offence, so is it an offence to
    tamper with the art of the stage director.

PLAYGOER: Then is all the stage direction of the world's plays worth-
    less?

STAGE DIRECTOR: Not to the reader, but to the stage director, and to
    the actor – yes.

PLAYGOER: But Shakespeare –

STAGE DIRECTOR: Shakespeare seldom directs the stage manager. Go
    through *Hamlet*, *Romeo and Juliet*, *King Lear*, *Othello*, any of the
    masterpieces, and except in some of the historical plays which contain
    descriptions of possessions, etc., what do you find? How are the
    scenes described in *Hamlet*?

PLAYGOER: My copy shows a clear description. It has 'Act I., scene i. Elsinore. A platform before the Castle.'

STAGE DIRECTOR: You are looking at a late edition with additions by a certain Mr Malone, but Shakespeare wrote nothing of the kind. His words are 'Actus primus. Scaena prima.' . . . And now let us look at *Romeo and Juliet*. What does your book say?

PLAYGOER: It says: 'Act I., scene i. Verona. A public place.'

STAGE DIRECTOR: And the second scene?

PLAYGOER: It says: 'Scene ii. A street.'

STAGE DIRECTOR: And the third scene?

PLAYGOER: It says: 'Scene iii. A room in Capulet's house.'

STAGE DIRECTOR: And now, would you like to hear what scene directions Shakespeare actually wrote for this play?

PLAYGOER: Yes.

STAGE DIRECTOR: He wrote: '*Actus primus. Scaena prima.*' And not another word as to act or scene throughout the whole play. And now for *King Lear*.

PLAYGOER: No, it is enough. I see now. Evidently Shakespeare relied upon the intelligence of the stage-men to complete their scene from his indication . . . But is this the same in regard to the actions? Does not Shakespeare place some descriptions through *Hamlet*, such as 'Hamlet leaps into Ophelia's grave', 'Laertes grapples with him', and later, 'The attendants part them, and they come out of the grave'?

STAGE DIRECTOR: No, not one word. All the stage directions, from the first to the last, are the tame inventions of sundry editors, Mr Malone, Mr Capell, Theobald and others, and they have committed an indiscretion in tampering with the play, for which we, the men of the theatre, have to suffer.

PLAYGOER: How is that?

STAGE DIRECTOR: Why, supposing any of us reading Shakespeare shall see in our mind's eye some other combination of movements contrary to the 'instructions' of these gentlemen, and suppose we represent our ideas on the stage, we are instantly taken to task by some knowing one, who accuses us of altering the directions of Shakespeare – nay more, of altering his very intentions.

PLAYGOER: But do not the 'knowing ones', as you call them, know that Shakespeare wrote no stage directions?

STAGE DIRECTOR: One can only guess that to be the case, to judge from their indiscreet criticisms. Anyhow, what I wanted to show you was that our greatest modern poet realised that to add stage directions was first of all unnecessary, and secondly, tasteless. We can therefore be sure that Shakespeare at any rate realised what was the work of the theatre craftsman – the stage manager, and that it was part of the stage manager's task to invent the scenes in which the play was to be set.

PLAYGOER: Yes, and you were telling me what each part consisted of.

STAGE DIRECTOR: Quite so. And now that we have disposed of the error that the author's directions are of any use, we can continue to speak of the way the stage-manager sets to work to interpret faithfully the play of the dramatist. I have said that he swears to follow the text faithfully, and that his first work is to read the play through and get the great impression; and in reading, as I have said, begins to see the whole colour, rhythm, action of the thing. He then puts the play aside for some time, and in his mind's eye mixes his palette (to use a painter's expression) with the colours which the impression of the play has called up. Therefore, on sitting down a second time to read through the play, he is surrounded by an atmosphere which he proposes to test. At the end of the second reading he will find that his more definite impressions have received clear and unmistakable corroboration, and that some of his impressions which were less positive have disappeared. He will then make a note of these. It is possible that he will even now commence to suggest, in line and colour, some of the scenes and ideas which are filling his head, but this is more likely to be delayed until he has re-read the play at least a dozen times.

PLAYGOER: But I thought the stage manager always left that part of the play – the scene designing – to the scene painter?

STAGE DIRECTOR: So he does, generally. First blunder of the modern theatre.

PLAYGOER: How is it a blunder?

STAGE DIRECTOR: This way: A has written a play which B promises to interpret faithfully. In so delicate a matter as the interpretation of so elusive a thing as the spirit of a play, which, do you think, will be the surest way to preseve the unity of that spirit? Will it be best if B does all the work by himself? or will it do to give the work into the hands of C, D and E, each of whom see or think differently to B or A?

PLAYGOER: Of course the former would be best. But is it possible for one man to do the work of three men?

STAGE DIRECTOR: That is the only way the work can be done, if unity, the one thing vital to a work of art, is to be obtained.

PLAYGOER: So, then, the stage manager does not call in a scene painter and ask him to design a scene, but he designs one himself?

STAGE DIRECTOR: Certainly. And remember he does not merely sit down and draw a pretty or historically accurate design, with enough doors and windows in picturesque places, but he first of all chooses certain colours which seem to him to be in harmony with the spirit of the play, rejecting other colours as out of tune. He then weaves into a pattern certain objects – an arch, a fountain, a balcony, a bed – using the chosen objects as the centre of his design. Then he adds to this all the objects which are mentioned in the play, and which are necessary to be seen. To these he adds, one by one, each character which appears in the play, and gradually each movement of each character, and each costume. He is as likely as not to make several mistakes in his pattern. If so, he must, as it were, unpick the design, and rectify the blunder even if he has to go right back to the beginning and start the pattern all over again – or he may even have to begin a new pattern. At any rate, slowly, harmoniously, must the whole design develop, so that the eye of the beholder shall be satisfied. While this pattern for the eye is being devised, the designer is being guided as much by the sound of the verse or prose as by the sense or spirit. And shortly all is prepared, and the actual work can be commenced.

PLAYGOER: What actual work? It seems to me that the stage-manager has already been doing a good deal of what may be called actual work.

STAGE DIRECTOR: Well, perhaps; but the difficulties have but commenced. By the actual work I mean the work which needs skilled labour, such as the actual painting of the huge spaces of canvas for the scenes, and the actual making of the costumes.

PLAYGOER: You are not going to tell me that the stage manager actually paints his own scenes and cuts his own costumes, and sews them together?

STAGE DIRECTOR: No, I will not say that he does so in every case and for every play, but he must have done so at one time or another during his apprenticeship, or must have closely studied all the technical points of these complicated crafts. Then will he be able to guide the skilled craftsmen in their different departments. And when the actual making of the scenes and costumes has commenced, the parts are distributed to the different actors, who learn the words before a single rehearsal takes place. (This as you may guess, is not the custom, but it is what should be seen to by a stage director such as I describe.) Meantime, the scenes and costumes are almost ready. I will not tell you the amount of interesting but laborious work it entails to prepare the play up to this point. But even when once the scenes are placed upon the stage, and the costumes upon the actors, the difficulty of the work is still great.

PLAYGOER: The stage director's work is not finished then?

STAGE DIRECTOR: Finished! What do you mean?

PLAYGOER: Well, I thought now that the scenes and costumes were all seen to, the actors and actresses would do the rest.

STAGE DIRECTOR: No, the stage manager's most interesting work is now beginning. His scene is set and his characters are clothed. He has, in short, a kind of dream picture in front of him. He clears the stage of all but the one, two, or more characters who are to commence the play, and he begins the scheme of lighting these figures and the scene.

PLAYGOER: What, is not this branch left to the discretion of the master electrician and his men?

STAGE DIRECTOR: The doing of it is left to them, but the manner of doing it is the business of the stage manager. Being, as I have said, a man of some intelligence and training, he has devised a special way of lighting his scene for this play, just as he has devised a special way of painting the scene and costuming the figures. If the word 'harmony' held no significance for him, he would of course leave it to the first comer.

PLAYGOER: Then do you actually mean that he has made so close a study of nature that he can direct his electricians how to make it appear as if the sun were shining at such and such an altitude, or as if the moonlight were flooding the interior of the room with such and such an intensity?

STAGE DIRECTOR: No, I should not like to suggest that, because the reproduction of nature's lights is not what my stage manager ever attempts. Neither should he attempt such an impossibility. Not to *reproduce* nature, but to *suggest* some of her most beautiful and most living ways – that is what my stage manager shall attempt. The other thing proclaims an overbearing assumption of omnipotence. A stage manager may well aim to be an artist, but it ill becomes him to attempt celestial honours. This attitude he can avoid by never trying to imprison or copy nature, for nature will be neither imprisoned nor allow any man to copy her with any success.

PLAYGOER: Then in what way does he set to work? What guides him in his task of lighting the scene and costumes which we are speaking about?

STAGE DIRECTOR: What guides him? Why, the scene and the

costumes, and the verse and the prose, and the sense of the play. All
these things, as I told you, have now been brought into harmony, the
one with the other – all goes smoothly – what simpler, then, that it
should so continue, and that the manager should be the only one to
know how to preserve this harmony which he has commenced to
create?

PLAYGOER: Will you tell me some more about the actual way of lighting the scene and the actors?

STAGE DIRECTOR: Certainly. What do you want to know?

PLAYGOER: Well, will you tell me why they put lights all along the
floor of the stage – footlights they call them, I believe?

STAGE DIRECTOR: Yes, footlights.

PLAYGOER: Well, why are they put on the ground?

STAGE DIRECTOR: It is one of the questions which has puzzled all
the theatre reform gentlemen, and none have been able to find an
answer, for the simple reason that there is no answer. There never
was an answer, there never will be an answer. The only thing to
do is to remove all the footlights out of all the theatres as quickly
as possible and say nothing about it. It is one of those queer things
which nobody can explain, and at which children are always surprised. Littly Nancy Lake, in 1812, went to Drury Lane Theatre,
and her father tells us that she also was astonished at the footlights. Said she:

> And there's a row of lamps, my eye!
> How they do blaze – I wonder why
> They keep them on the ground.
> – *Rejected Addresses*

That was in 1812! and we are still wondering.

PLAYGOER: A friend of mine – an actor – once told me that if there
were no footlights all the faces of the actors would look dirty.

STAGE DIRECTOR: That was the remark of a man who did not
understand that in place of the footlights another method of lighting
the faces and figures could be adopted. It is this simple kind of thing
which never occurs to those people who will not devote a little time
to even a slight study of the other branches of the craft.

PLAYGOER: Do not the actors study the other crafts of the theatre?

STAGE DIRECTOR: As a rule – no, and in some ways it is opposed to
the very life of an actor. If an actor of intelligence were to devote
much time to the study of all the branches of the theatrical art he
would gradually cease to act, and would end by becoming a stage

manager – so absorbing is the whole art in comparison with the single craft of acting.

PLAYGOER: My friend the actor also added that if the footlights were removed the audience would not be able to see the expression of his face.

STAGE DIRECTOR: Had Henry Irving or Eleanora Duse said so, the remark would have had some meaning. The ordinary actor's face is either so violently expressive or violently inexpressive, that it would be a blessing if the theatres were not only without footlights but without any lights at all. By the way, an excellent theory of the origin of the footlights is advanced by M. Ludovic Celler in *Les Decors, les costumes et la mise en-scéne au XVII. siécle.* The usual way of lighting the stage was by means of large chandeliers, circular or triangular, which were suspended above the heads of the actors and the audience; and M. Celler is of the opinion that the system of footlights owes its origin to the small plain theatres which could not afford to have chandeliers, and therefore placed tallow candles on the floor in front of the stage. I believe this theory to be correct, for common sense could not have dictated such an artistic blunder; whereas the box-office receipts may easily have done so. Remember how little artistic virtue is in the box-office! When we have time I will tell you some things about this same powerful usurper of the theatrical throne – the box-office. But let us return to a more serious and a more interesting topic than this lack of expression and this footlight matter. We had passed in review the different tasks of the stage manager – scene, costume, lighting – and we had come to the most interesting part, that of the manipulation of the figures in all their movements and speeches. You expressed astonishment that the acting – that is to say, the speaking and actions of the actors – was not left to the actors to arrange for themselves. But consider for an instant the nature of this work. Would you have that which has already grown into a certain unified pattern, suddenly spoiled by the addition of something accidental?

PLAYGOER: How do you mean? I understand what you suggest, but will you not show me more exactly how the actor can spoil the pattern?

STAGE DIRECTOR: *Unconsciously* spoil it, mind you! I do not for an instant mean that it is his wish to be out of harmony with his surroundings, but he does so through innocence. Some actors have the right instincts in this matter, and some have none whatever. But even those whose instincts are most keen cannot remain in the pattern, cannot be harmonious, without following the directions of the stage manager.

PLAYGOER: Then you do not even permit the leading actor and actress to move and act as their instincts and reason dictate?

STAGE DIRECTOR: No, rather must they be the very first to follow the direction of the stage manager, so often do they become the very centre of the pattern – the very heart of the emotional design.

PLAYGOER: And is that understood and appreciated by them?

STAGE DIRECTOR: Yes, but only when they realise and appreciate at the same time that the play, and the right and just interpretation of the play, is the all-important thing in the modern theatre. Let me illustrate this point to you. The play to be presented is *Romeo and Juliet*. We have studied the play, prepared scene and costume, lighted both, and now our rehearsals for the actors commence. The first movement of the great crowd of unruly citizens of Verona, fighting, swearing, killing each other, appals us. It horrifies us that in this white little city of roses and song and love there should dwell this amazing and detestable hate which is ready to burst out at the very church doors, or in the middle of the May festival, or under the windows of the house of a newly born girl. Quickly following on this picture, and even while we remember the ugliness which larded both faces of Capulet and Montague, there comes strolling down the road the son of Montague, our Romeo, who is soon to be lover and the loved of his Juliet. Therefore, whoever is chosen to move and speak as Romeo must move and speak as part and parcel of the design – this design which I have already pointed out to you as having a definite form. He must move across our sight in a certain way, passing to a certain point, in a certain light, his head at a certain angle, his eyes, his feet, his whole body in tune with the play, and not (as is often the case) in tune with his own thoughts only, and these out of harmony with the play. For his thoughts (beautiful as they may chance to be) may not match the spirit or the pattern which has been so carefully prepared by the director.

PLAYGOER: Would you have the stage manager control the movements of whoever might be impersonating the character of Romeo, even if he were a fine actor?

STAGE DIRECTOR: Most certainly; and the finer the actor the finer his intelligence and taste, and therefore the more easily controlled. In fact, I am speaking in particular of a theatre wherein all the actors are men of refinement and the manager a man of peculiar accomplishments.

PLAYGOER: But are you not asking these intelligent actors almost to become puppets?

STAGE DIRECTOR: A sensitive question! which one would expect from an actor who felt uncertain about his powers. A puppet is at present only a doll, delightful enough for a puppet show. But for a theatre we need more than a doll. Yet that is the feeling which some actors have about their relationship with the stage manager. They feel they are having their strings pulled, and resent it, and show they feel hurt – insulted.

PLAYGOER: I can understand that.

STAGE DIRECTOR: And cannot you also understand that they should be willing to be controlled? Consider for a moment the relationship of the men on a ship, and you will understand what I consider to be the relationship of men in a theatre. Who are the workers on a ship?

PLAYGOER: A ship? Why, there is the captain, the commander, the first, second and third lieutenants, the navigation officer, and so on, and the crew.

STAGE DIRECTOR: Well, and what is it that guides the ship?

PLAYGOER: The rudder?

STAGE DIRECTOR: Yes, and what else?

PLAYGOER: The steersman who holds the wheel of the rudder.

STAGE DIRECTOR: And who else?

PLAYGOER: The man who controls the steersman.

STAGE DIRECTOR: And who is that?

PLAYGOER: The navigation officer.

STAGE DIRECTOR: And who controls the navigation officer?

PLAYGOER: The captain.

STAGE DIRECTOR: And are any orders which do not come from the captain, or by his authority, obeyed?

PLAYGOER: No, they should not be.

STAGE DIRECTOR: And can the ship steer its course in safety without the captain?

PLAYGOER: It is not usual.

STAGE DIRECTOR: And do the crew obey the captain and his officers?

PLAYGOER: Yes, as a rule.

STAGE DIRECTOR: Willingly?

PLAYGOER: Yes.

STAGE DIRECTOR: And is that not called discipline?

PLAYGOER: Yes.

STAGE DIRECTOR: And discipline – what is that the result of?

PLAYGOER: The proper and willing subjection to rules and principles.

STAGE DIRECTOR: And the first of those principles is obedience, is it not?

PLAYGOER: It is.

STAGE DIRECTOR: Very well, then. It will not be difficult for you to understand that a theatre in which so many hundred persons are engaged at work is in many respects like a ship, and demands like management. And it will not be difficult for you to see how the slightest sign of disobedience would be disastrous. Mutiny has been well anticipated in the navy, but not in the theatre. The navy has taken care to define, in clear and unmistakable voice, that the captain of the vessel is the king, and a despotic ruler into the bargain. Mutiny on a ship is dealt with by a court-martial, and is put down by very severe punishment, by imprisonment, or by dismissal from the service.

PLAYGOER: But you are not going to suggest such a possibility for the theatre?

STAGE DIRECTOR: The theatre, unlike the ship, is not made for purposes of war, and so for some unaccountable reason discipline is not held to be of such vital importance, whereas it is of as much importance as in any branch of service. But what I wish to show you is that until discipline is understood in a theatre to be willing and reliant obedience to the manager or captain no supreme achievement can be accomplished.

PLAYGOER: But are not the actors, scene-men, and the rest all willing workers?

STAGE DIRECTOR: Why, my dear friend, there never were such glorious natured people as these men and women of the theatre. They are enthusiastically willing, but sometimes their judgement is at fault, and they become as willing to be unruly as to be obedient, and as willing to lower the standard as to raise it. As for nailing the flag to the mast – this is seldom dreamed of – for *compromise* and the vicious doctrine of compromise with the enemy is preached by the officers of the theatrical navy. Our enemies are vulgar display, the lower public opinion, and ignorance. To these our 'officers' wish us to knuckle under. What the theatre people have not yet quite comprehended is *the value of a high standard and the value of a director who abides by it.*

PLAYGOER: And that director, why should he not be an actor or a scene-painter?

STAGE DIRECTOR: Do you pick your leader from the ranks, exalt him to be captain, and then let him handle the guns and the ropes? No; the director of a theatre must be a man apart from any of the crafts. He must be a man who knows but no longer handles the ropes.

PLAYGOER: But I believe it is a fact that many well-known leaders in the theatres have been actors and stage managers at the same time?

STAGE DIRECTOR: Yes, that is so. But you will not find it easy to assure me that no mutiny was heard of under their rule. Right away from all this question of positions there is the question of the art, the work. If an actor assumes the management of the stage, and if he is a better actor than his fellows, a natural instinct will lead him to make himself the centre of everything. He will feel that unless he does so the work will appear thin and unsatisfying. He will pay less heed to the play than he will to his own part, and he will, in fact, gradually cease to look upon the work as a whole. And this is not good for the work. This is not the way a work of art is to be produced in the theatre.

PLAYGOER: But might it not be possible to find a great actor who would be so great an artist that as manager he would never do as you say, but who would handle himself as actor, just the same as he handles the rest of the material?

STAGE DIRECTOR: All things are possible, but firstly, it is against the nature of an actor to do as you suggest; secondly, it is against the nature of the stage manager to perform; and thirdly, it is against all nature that a man can be in two places at once. Now, the place of the actor is on the stage, in a certain position, ready by means of his brains to give suggestions of certain emotions, surrounded by certain scenes and people; and it is the place of the stage manager to be in front of this, that he may view it as a whole. So that you see even if we found our perfect actor who was our perfect stage manager, he could not be in two places at the same time. Of course we have sometimes seen the conductor of a small orchestra playing the part of the first violin, but not from choice, and not to a satisfactory issue; neither is it the practice in large orchestras.

PLAYGOER: I understand, then, that you would allow no one to rule on the stage except the stage manager?

STAGE DIRECTOR: The nature of the work permits nothing else.

PLAYGOER: Not even the playwright?

STAGE DIRECTOR: Only when the playwright has practised and studied the crafts of acting, scene-painting, costume, lighting, and dance, not otherwise. But playwrights, who have not been cradled in the theatre, generally know little of these crafts. Goethe, whose love

for the theatre remained ever fresh and beautiful, was in many ways
one of the greatest of stage directors. But, when he linked himself
to the Weimar theatre, he forgot to do what the great musician who
followed him remembered. Goethe permitted an authority in the
theatre higher than himself, that is to say, the owner of the theatre.
Wagner was careful to possess himself of his theatre, and become a
sort of feudal baron in his castle.

PLAYGOER: Was Goethe's failure as a theatre director due to this
fact?

STAGE DIRECTOR: Obviously, for had Goethe held the keys of the
doors that impudent little poodle would never have got as far as its
dressing-room; the leading lady would never have made the theatre
and herself immortally ridiculous; and Weimar would have been
saved the tradition of having perpetrated the most shocking blunder
which ever occurred inside a theatre.

PLAYGOER: The traditions of most theatres certainly do not seem to
show that the artist is held in much respect on the stage.

STAGE DIRECTOR: Well, it would be easy to say a number of hard
things about the theatre and its ignorance of art. But one does not hit
a thing which is down, unless, perhaps, with the hope that the shock
may cause it to leap to its feet again. And our Western theatre is very
much down. The East still boasts a theatre. Ours here in the West is
on its last legs. But I look for a Renaissance.

PLAYGOER: How will that come?

STAGE DIRECTOR: Through the advent of a man who shall contain in
him all the qualities which go to make up a master of the theatre,
and through the reform of the theatre as an instrument. When that is
accomplished, when the theatre has become a masterpiece of mechanism, when it has invented a technique, it will without any effort
develop a *creative art* of its own. But the whole question of the development of the craft into a self-reliant and creative art would take
too long to go thoroughly into at present. There are already some
theatre men at work on the building of the theatres; some are reforming the acting, some the scenery. And all of this must be of
some small value. But the very first thing to be realised is that little
or no result can come from the reforming of a single craft of the
theatre without at the same time, in the same theatre, reforming all
the other crafts. *The whole renaissance of the Art of the Theatre depends
upon the extent that this is realised.* The Art of the Theatre, as I have
already told you, is divided up into so many crafts: acting, scene,
costume, lighting, carpentering, singing, dancing, etc., that it must

be realised at the commencement that ENTIRE, not PART reform is needed; and it must be realised that *one* part, one craft, has a *direct* bearing upon each of the other crafts in the theatre, and that no result can come from fitful, uneven reform, but only from a systematic progression. Therefore, the reform of the Art of the Theatre is possible to those men alone who have studied and practised all the crafts of the theatre.

PLAYGOER: That is to say, your ideal stage manager.

STAGE DIRECTOR: Yes. You will remember that at the commencement of our conversation I told you my belief in the Renaissance of the Art of the Theatre was based in my belief in the Renaissance of the stage director, and that when he had understood the right use of actors, scene, costume, lighting, and dance, and by means of these had mastered the crafts of interpretation, he would then gradually acquire the mastery of action, line, colour, rhythm, and words, this last strength developing out of all the rest. . . . Then I said the Art of the Theatre would have won back its rights, and its work would stand self-reliant as a creative art, and no longer as an interpretative craft.

PLAYGOER: Yes, and at the time I did not quite understand what you meant, and though I can now understand your drift, I do not quite in my mind's eye see the stage without its poet.

STAGE DIRECTOR: What? Shall anything be lacking when the poet shall no longer write for the theatre?

PLAYGOER: The play will be lacking.

STAGE DIRECTOR: Are you sure of that?

PLAYGOER: Well, the play will certainly not exist if the poet or playwright is not there to write it.

STAGE DIRECTOR: There will not be any play in the sense in which you use the word.

PLAYGOER: But you propose to present something to the audience, and I presume before you are able to present them with that something you must have it in your possession.

STAGE DIRECTOR: Certainly; you could not have made a surer remark. Where you are at fault is to take for granted, as if it were a law for the Medes and Persians, that that *something* must be made of words.

PLAYGOER: Well, what is this something which is not words, but for presentation to the audience?

STAGE DIRECTOR: First tell me, is not an idea something?

PLAYGOER: Yes, but it lacks form.

STAGE DIRECTOR: Well, but is it not permissible to give an idea whatever form the artist chooses?

PLAYGOER: Yes.

STAGE DIRECTOR: And is it an unpardonable crime for the theatrical artist to use some different material to the poet's?

PLAYGOER: No.

STAGE DIRECTOR: Then we are permitted to attempt to give form to an idea in whatever material we find or invent, provided it is not a material which should be put to a better use?

PLAYGOER: Yes.

STAGE DIRECTOR: Very good; follow what I have to say for the next few minutes, and then go home and think about it for a while. Since you have granted all I asked you to permit, I am now going to tell you out of what material an artist of the theatre of the future will create his masterpieces. Out of ACTION, SCENE and VOICE. Is it not very simple?

And when I say *action*, I mean both gesture and dancing, the prose and poetry of action.

When I say *scene*, I mean all which comes before the eye, such as the lighting, costume, as well as the scenery.

When I say *voice*, I mean the spoken word or the word which is sung, in contradiction to the word which is read, for the word written to be spoken and the word written to be read are two entirely different things.

And now, though I have but repeated what I told you at the beginning of our conversation, I am delighted to see that you no longer look so puzzled.

3. Actors and Acting

Craig lost interest in being an actor. Despite looks and a physique which fitted him for playing the leading classical roles, he parted company with acting with equanimity. In *Index to the Story of My Days* he recalled how he began to find lines harder to learn, for all he was still a young man, and how indifference set in for which in retrospect he was heartily grateful.

He had learned the business of acting by being thrust onto the stage of the Lyceum at the age of seventeen in a melodrama called *The Dead Heart*, and was astute enough to realise his own deficiencies. Irving appreciated that playing minor parts, even in his company, was going to prove insufficient encouragement for Craig and made no attempt to stand in his way when offers arrived to take leading parts on tour. There was something in Craig's disposition which inclined him to dramatise his life off-stage as well as on, and it took but a few years for him to become aware of the gulf between his own immature reactions to the world around him, and the art of the actor.

I say 'the art of the actor' despite the declaration in *The Actor and the Über-marionette* that acting is not an art and that therefore the actor cannot be termed an artist. Much later he was to refer to this remark as clear evidence that he at least was not an actor because an actor would have been unable to understand what it meant.

It is necessary to balance this apparent disdain for the actor and his profession both against his hopes for a new kind of actor and his enormous admiration for Henry Irving. In his book on Irving published in 1930 Craig offered an account of Irving's style more graphic and illuminating than any to be found elsewhere. The description of Irving in *The Bells* is often regarded as Craig's best piece of prose writing. It is also too long to include here without unbalancing the historical element in what is not intended as a historical survey. Craig devotes a whole chapter to Irving's vocal mannerisms and peculiarities of gait, whose eccentricity were a source of annoyance to the sterner critics. He also identifies Irving's quality as a performer, and it is this, most of all, which seems to have intrigued him.

When he later maintained that Irving was the nearest he ever saw to the Über-marionette it was the highest compliment he could pay. It was, of course, onto the notion of the actor as little more than a puppet that Craig's detractors have most gleefully leeched, and he was several times forced in later times to amplify his meaning.

At one level he wished not to rid the theatre of its actors and actresses – though he did suggest that his school should be for men only – but to promote a theatre in which it was possible for the actor to offer his intelligence and his imagination rather than simply his passion. When he ridiculed the conceit of Shakespeare writing *Othello* in a fit of jealousy, his example was unfair. The actor cannot react with the detachment of the playwright. The argument that the actor should have his 'brain commanding his nature', on the other hand, is as clear an exposition of the Brechtian principle as one could hope to find, and pre-dates Brecht by twenty years.

That it should be Irving who is singled out as the supreme example of this ideal of an actor might indicate perhaps that the gulf between the nineteenth and the twentieth centuries, between 'old' movements and 'new', is one that can always be bridged by special talent. Craig's work with Stanislavsky and Sulerjhitsky in the preparation of *Hamlet* for the Moscow Art Theatre occupied several years during which the three men pooled ideas, and acknowledged their differences. The Russians made most of the compromises. Stanislavsky's system of acting was still in a formative stage. The actors were not fully aware of what it involved, nor, it would seem, were Stanislavsky and Sulerjhitsky. Productions at the Moscow Art Theatre were no longer necessarily rooted in the principles of Naturalism but the actors were encouraged to locate their performances strictly within the bounds of psychological realism. Craig's vision of the character of Hamlet and the corruption of the Court could be accommodated as a production process without serious upset. Even the famous screens whose construction proved so problematical were more consonant with Russian staging practice than that of Germany or England when Craig had offered non-realistic settings to Otto Brahm and Beerbohm Tree. For the Moscow *Hamlet* the physical factors took a deal of working out, but served as a source of inspiration to Stanislavsky.

What Craig could not accommodate was the acting of the company and as Stanislavsky handled most of the rehearsals in Craig's continued absence, the chance of doing something about it never arose: hence the

dissatisfaction with the whole enterprise later voiced by Craig. In his
attack in *Stanislavsky's System*, he exempts the actor Artem from criti-
cism because his ability transcended the System. An actor like Artem, a
'born actor' was, Craig implies, too good for the System. The condem-
nation of *An Actor Prepares* as 'a book for excellent dummies who
would like to be famous and probably will be, without ever coming to
act like true actors', is less of a surprise than many of the attitudes Craig
strikes, and does imply that he had not greatly modified his opinions
since the plea in *The Actor and the Über-marionette* for an actor who
will represent rather than impersonate.

The vision of the actor of his own time as a prey to his own personality and to the adulation of his admirers is no new one. Stage
reformers of every period have bemoaned the seductive aspect of a
profession which offers an easier path for the idle and self-satisfied.
Craig required more. He asked for a revolution in acting techniques
that would revive the necessary discipline of masked acting in classical
Athens and restore 'noble artificiality'. This is why with customary
hyperbole he asserted that 'the actor must go, and in his place comes
the inanimate figure – the Über-marionette we may call him, until he
has won for himself a better name'.

In *A Durable Theatre* Craig talks again of the Über-marionette and
refers to an oriental tradition of theatre. It is here that we should look
for a living example of Craig's desire to raise the actor above the level
of everyday behaviour. Artaud too found something in the theatre of
the East to inspire him when dancers from Bali visited Paris for the
first time, and his dream was surely close to Craig's when he wrote of
the actor as 'a martyr burnt at the stake signalling through the flames'.
Javanese masked dance, the *wayang topeng*, is closely akin in stance and
gesture to the puppet form of the *wayang golek* and even the shadow
puppet, the *wayang purwa*. In the discipline of these forms and those
of the classical dance of India, the Noh and Kabuki of Japan and the
Pekin Opera, it becomes possible to comprehend something of Craig's
ideal.

Whether or not this ever can or ever could be translated to Western
theatre is another matter. Meyerhold flirted with a theatre of sculptural
gesture but ended up with Biomechanics, which tended to reduce the
actor rather than promote him, while Brecht rejected 'impersonation'
and 'representation', but never aimed at what Craig would have identified as 'creation'.

Perhaps Craig's approach to theatre as a visual artist was too dominant
for him ever to be satisfied with the actor. Perhaps, on the other hand,

placing the value he did on movement and line, he might, through the medium of his school – modern terminology would call it a 'workshop' – have been able to create a new theatre of his own in which the actor did have a vital and satisfying part to play.

from *Index to the Story of My Days* (1956)

In the histories of actors one gets their temperaments compared, their way of speaking 'To be or not to be', the way they fought a duel in *The Corsican Brothers*: everything, in fact, is compared except their physical appearance. I have never been able to find out whether Burbage was tall or short, whether Betterton was short or tall. Garrick, we hear, was half and half; Kean was on the short side, I believe. Irving was tall. But I think it would be quite interesting if we had a diagram showing the relative sizes of actors, with their measurements, just as we are told the relative quantity of sheep bred in Australia and Canada. This should be done not only with tragedians – though I have mentioned only these – but with comedians too. A rough way of thinking of the two groups is that tragedians are muscular and tall and comedians are small and round.

This came to my mind when thinking of the only time I saw Irving, our great tragedian, with one of the great comedians of the epoch – with Little Tich. Looking at their faces, you could see that the one was quite as serious as the other, and certainly quite as tragic. Little Tich was not jumping about or making grimaces; he was, like Grock when he is off the stage, a very serious man. Grock, before he gets more than half of his make-up on, always reminds me of Picasso – I suppose the resemblance has struck many people. Well, the spectacle of Irving standing beside Little Tich on the steps of the Mitre Hotel at Hampton Court on the day of, or the day after, Queen Victoria's Jubilee, was not to be easily forgotten. I daresay the sufferings those two underwent, before each of them reached the position he did, were very similar. I wonder what ambition drove Little Tich to become, as he did, a Continental clown of the very best kind. Paris audiences welcomed him because they understood his kind of fun. The audience at the Folies Bergères used to be, I think, the most strikingly serious audience I ever looked at. I often liked to turn and look long at the audience there. Such faces, I thought, and such expressions, would be appropriate to the profoundest readers of the work of Plato or Erasmus. And in the music halls in England were faces equally serious, as they watched Dan Leno, for instance? Dan Leno, by the by, seems to be utterly forgotten.

As Grock will be now that he has retired – though Grock retires
wealthy, comfortable, apparently very sure of himself and in perfect
health. Whereas poor Dan Leno was a wreck and had to be nursed.

from *Henry Irving* (1930)

Irving can be said to have been essentially a traditional actor. Although
he broke with a number of ridiculous English conventions, decayed
traditions that were obviously not worth preserving, or traditions that
did not suit his purpose, he never broke with any of the noble ancient
traditions. . . .

All the caricaturists attributed to Irving bent knees, bent back, or a
dragging leg – like the aesthete in *Iolanthe* – which, if not particularly
funny, was anyhow quite untrue.

For no one walked so well. Actors as a rule walk with precision and
grace, and all who saw him will tell you that Irving walked perfectly
naturally – but only in private life. As he stepped upon the boards of
his theatre, at rehearsal, something was added to the walk – a consci-
ousness. And this was right. He became aware of the boards; the ordinary life was being put away; something was coming into his blood;
he could not feel the same as when on the paving stones of Bond
Street . . .

But if, to Irving's ordinary walk in daily life, a springing motion was
added at rehearsal, it was only a forecast of what was to come at night
. . . It wasn't walking. It was dancing!

In dancing his role, Irving went to the extreme limits possible to an
actor of the nineteenth century, of preserving the last tingle of the
mighty Greek tradition . . . He danced, he did not merely walk – he
sang, he by no means merely spoke. He was essentially artificial in
distinction to being merely natural . . .

Every now and again the words were natural, but as a rule they were
more than natural – they were highly artifical. And thus it came about
that Irving positively designed (as M. Fokine has designed) dances
which fitted perfectly to the speeches given him by Shakespeare.

When he came to melodrama, to *The Bells*, *The Lyons Mail*, or *Louis
XI*, he realised that a good deal more dance would be needed to hold up
these pieces – and then it was that, putting out all his skill, he wiped
the floor with the role and danced it like the devil. When it was Shakespeare he was dealing with, he had merely to wipe the beautiful glass
window-panes. His movements were all measured. He was for ever
counting – one, two, three – pause – one, two – a step, another, a halt, a

faintest turn, another step, a word. (Call it a beat, a foot, a step, all is one – I like to use the word 'step'.) That constituted one of his dances. Or seated on a chair, at a table – raising a glass, drinking – and then lowering his hand and glass – one, two, three, four – suspense – a slight step with his eyes – five – then a patter of steps – two slow syllables – another step – two more syllables – and a second passage in his dance was done. And so right through the piece – whatever it might be – there was no chance movement; he left no loose ends . . .

From the first to the last moment that Irving stood on the stage each moment was significant . . . every sound, each movement, was intentional – clear-cut, measured dance: nothing real – all massively artificial – yet all flashing with the light and the pulse of nature. A fine style.

from *The Artists of the Theatre of the Future* (1908)

ON THE ACTOR

As a man he ranks high, possesses generosity, and the truest sense of comradeship. I call to mind one actor whom I know and who shall stand as the type. A genial companion, and spreading a sense of companionship in the theatre; generous in giving assistance to younger and less accomplished actors, continually speaking about the work, picturesque in his manner, able to hold his own when standing at the side of the stage instead of in the centre; with a voice which commands my attention when I hear it, and finally, with about as much knowledge of the art as a cuckoo has of anything which is at all constructive. Anything to be made according to plan or design is foreign to his nature. But his good nature tells him that others are on the stage besides himself, and that there must be a certain feeling of unity between their thoughts and his, yet this arrives by a kind of good natured instinct and not through knowledge, and produces nothing positive. Instinct and experience have taught him a few things, I am not going to call them tricks, which he continually repeats. For instance, he has learned that the sudden drop in the voice from forte to piano has the power of accentuating and thrilling the audience as much as the crescendo from the piano into the forte. He also knows that laughter is capable of very many sounds, and not merely Ha Ha Ha. He knows that geniality is a rare thing on the stage and that the bubbling personality is always welcomed. But what he does not know is this, that this same bubbling personality and all this same instinctive knowledge doubles or even trebles its power when guided by scientific knowledge, that is to say, by art. If he should hear

me say this now he would be lost in amazement and would consider
that I was saying something which was finicking, dry, and not at all for
the consideration of an artist. He is one who thinks that emotion creates
emotion, and hates anything to do with calculation. It is not necessary
for me to point out that all art has to do with calculation and that the
man who disregards this can only be but half an actor. Nature will not
alone supply all which goes to create a work of art, for it is not the
privilege of trees, mountains and brooks to create works of art, or
everything which they touch would be given a definite and beautiful
form. It is the particular power which belongs to man alone, and to him
through his intelligence and his will. My friend probably thinks that
Shakespeare wrote *Othello* in a passion of jealousy and that all he had to
do was to write the first words which came into his mouth; but I am of
the opinion, and I think others hold the same opinion, that the words
had to pass through our author's head and that it was just through this
process and through the quality of his imagination and the strength of
his brain that the richness of his nature was able to be entirely and
clearly expressed, and by no other process could he have arrived at this.

Therefore it follows that the actor who wishes to perform *Othello*,
let us say, must have not only the rich nature from which to draw his
wealth, but must also have the imagination to know what to bring forth,
and the brain to know how to put it before us. Therefore the ideal
actor will be the man who possesses both a rich nature and a powerful
brain. Of his nature we need not speak. It will contain everything. Of
his brain we can say that the finer the brain the less liberty will it allow
itself, remembering how much depends upon its co-worker, the emotion, and also the less liberty will it allow its fellow-worker knowing
how valuable to it is its sternest control. Finally, the intellect would
bring both itself and the emotions to so fine a sense of reason that the
work would never boil to the bubbling point with its restless exhibition
of activity, but would create that perfect moderate heat which it would
know how to keep temperate. The perfect actor would be he whose
brain could conceive and could show us the perfect symbols of all
which his nature contains. He would not ramp and rage up and down in
Othello, rolling his eyes and clenching his hands in order to give us an
impression of jealousy; he would tell his brain to enquire into the depths,
to learn all that lies there, and then to remove itself to another sphere,
the sphere of the imagination, and there fashion certain symbols which,
without exhibiting the bare passions, would none the less tell us clearly
about them. And the perfect actor who should do this would in time
find out that the symbols are to be made mainly from material which

lies outside his person. But I will speak to you fully about this when I get to the end of our talk. For then I shall show you that the actor as he is today, must ultimately disappear and be merged in something else if works of art are to be seen in our kingdom of the theatre.

Meantime do not forget that the very nearest approach that has ever been to the ideal actor, with his brain commanding his nature, has been Henry Irving. There are many books which tell you about him, and the best of all the books is his face. Procure all the pictures, photographs, drawings, you can of him, and try to read what is there. To begin with you will find a mask, and the significance of this is most important. I think you will find it difficult to say when you look on the face, that it betrays the weaknesses which may have been in the nature. Try and conceive for yourself that face in movement – movement which was ever under the powerful control of the mind. Can you not see the mouth being made to move by the brain, and that same movement which is called expression creating a thought as definite as the line of a draughtsman does on a piece of paper or as a chord does in music? Cannot you see the slow turning of those eyes and the enlargement of them? These two movements alone contained so great a lesson for the future of the art of the theatre, pointed out so clearly the right use of expression as opposed to the wrong use, that it is amazing to me that many people have not seen more clearly what the future must be. I should say that the face of Irving was the connecting link between that spasmodic and ridiculous expression of the human face as used by the theatres of the last few centuries, and the masks which will be used in place of the human face in the near future.

Try and think of all this when losing hope that you will ever bring your nature as exhibited in your face and your person under sufficient command. Know for a truth that there is something other than your face and your person which you may use and which is easier to control. Know this, but make no attempt yet awhile to close with it. Continue to be an actor, continue to learn all that has to be learned, as to how they set about controlling the face, and then you will learn finally that it is not to be entirely controlled.

I give you this hope so that when this moment arrives you will not do as the other actors have done. They have been met by this difficulty and have shirked it, have compromised, and have not dared to arrive at the conclusion which an artist must arrive at if faithful to himself. That is to say, that the mask is the only right medium of portraying the expressions of the soul as shown through the expressions of the face.

from *A Letter to Ellen Terry* (1908)

Can acting ever be taught? No; you've said so hundreds of times. NO.
But though you have never claimed the laurel of the critic, still you
are quite right, you must be. Don't you mean that you cannot teach
acting as you can teach the rules of proportion, or as you can teach
counterpoint? These things have laws which hold good for all artists,
architects and musicians, and by following which a decently musical or
artistic being can create beautiful harmonies, pictures or buildings, but
by disregarding which can be created hideous confusion.

'I know, my dear, I know.' A gentle and a sweet sniff, a raising of
the head as if looking far into the distance, and in your movements I
hear your answer.

But how right you are, how entirely right. Acting cannot be taught.
And as it cannot be taught, acting will ever remain one of those beautiful
chance products which seldom are seen in their full beauty. How many
times in a century is it seen? Six or eight? I dare say you in your generosity
would say ten. And how many actors are there in the world today?

I am just now writing a fearsome looking essay which commences,
'Acting is not an art. Actors are not artists', and the rest of it. Now
that's a bright way to begin, but when you read it, you will know what
it all means. You will know that I am following up that which you
assert – that acting cannot be taught, that it has not laws; that, obviously,
if this is true it is no art.

I think if it had any laws you would have found them out long
ago, and would have told me. Then what also supports what I
advance is the fact that Madame Duse speaks in something of the
same strain, saying that until all the actors die of the plague the stage
will not be saved. As you know, she goes on to say, 'They poison
the air, they make art impossible'; and she probably includes herself
– don't you think so? – because she is not vain or stupid. She probably means that to stop acting altogether, and for the theatre to be
thoroughly swept out – brushing aside all the plays, all the costumes
and the rest of the Lord Mayor's Show – would leave the place so
blank and so fresh in its emptiness that when the people of the
theatre once more entered it they would enter in a different spirit,
and in royal trim; courage up, pride up, and purpose fixed; and with
those qualities behind them they would be in a condition to create
works of their own without assistance of the playwright, of the cos-
tumer or of the orchestra. I think that is her opinion. The staff on

which her flag waves has no end. The flag can go up and up without reaching the top. I believe that the great actors possess the power of creating pieces of work without assistance from anyone else; that is to say, I believe that you, or one of the few others, could, taking some theme or some two themes – let us say the idea of meeting and the idea of parting – out of these things, by movement, scene and voice, put before the audience all the different meanings of all the joys and sorrows that are wrapped up in the idea of meeting and the idea of parting. Especially could a woman do this.

Let us, as it were, now make such a piece. We search in our imagination, or in our memory, or wherever it is to be found, for the vision of those particular places where meetings happen. We gather them all together, ten, twenty, forty, a hundred. Some we throw away as valueless. Those which we have retained, those which we have selected, we put down, either in our memory if we are clever enough, or in writing, or, better still, with a few touches of the brush or pencil on paper. Those which we have selected mean so much to us that when they are set before an audience, in the right way, they will mean as much to them. They cannot fail to do so. So far so good.

We next picture to ourselves, or call up from our remembrance, from the thousand and one sources – books, pictures, and what we will – those exquisite and appealing movements which anticipated a meeting, and which lay in the very meeting itself. We recall to mind, or, appealing to our imagination, we meditate long, and we beseech it to remind us of all those sounds which are connected with this theme. Not merely sounds of the voice, but those sounds innumerable by which even a blind man can tell what is happening and what is about to happen, as clearly as if he could see it.

Having got together this material, these three separate collections, as it were, of things done, things seen, things heard (and even while we were collecting them we have been particular to put aside and commingle only those which were of the same family), we can say we have gathered together so many harmonies in movement, scene and voice on this theme. We know that no artist will express these in the same way, and in the expression is the indefinable quality which here cannot be talked about. One will make his movements symbolical, another will make them realistic. One will make his scenes a vision, retaining only the very essence of the ideas which he has gathered together; another will make his a realistic scene. One will utter sounds musical in their quality, and will convey a sense – a *hint* of the thing; and another will state facts, using matter-of-fact words; and in either case success can be attained, although the finer success comes with the imaginative treatment.

from *The Actor and The Über-marionette* (1907)

'To save the theatre, the theatre must be destroyed, the actors and actresses must all die of the plague. . . . They make art impossible.' (Eleanora Duse: *Studies in Seven Arts*, Arthur Symons.)

It has always been a matter for argument whether or no acting is an art, and therefore whether the actor is an artist, or something quite different. There is little to show us that this question disturbed the minds of the leaders of thought at any period, though there is much evidence to prove that had they chosen to approach this subject as one for their serious consideration, they would have applied to it the same method of inquiry as used when considering the arts of music and poetry, of architecture, sculpture and painting.

On the other hand there have been many warm arguments in certain circles on this topic. Those taking part in it have seldom been actors, very rarely men of the theatre at all, and all have displayed any amount of illogical heat and very little knowledge of the subject. The arguments against acting being an art, and against the actor being an artist, are generally so unreasonable and so personal in their detestation of the actor, that I think it is for this reason the actors have taken no trouble to go into the matter. So now regularly with each season comes the quarterly attack on the actor and on his jolly calling; the attack usually ending in the retirement of the enemy. As a rule it is the literary or private gentlemen who fill the enemy's rank. On the strength of having gone to see plays all their lives, or on the strength of never having gone to see a play in their lives, they attack for some reason best known to themselves. I have followed these regular attacks season by season, and they seem mostly to spring from irritability, personal enmity, or conceit. They are illogical from beginning to end. There can be no such attack made on the actor or his calling. My intention here is not to join in any such attempt; I would merely place before you what seem to me to be the logical facts of a curious case, and I believe that these admit of no dispute whatever.

Acting is not an art. It is therefore incorrect to speak of the actor as an artist. For accident is an enemy of the artist. Art is the exact antithesis of pandemonium, and pandemonium is created by the tumbling together of many accidents. Art arrives only by design. Therefore in order to make any work of art it is clear we may only work in those materials with which we can calculate. Man is not one of these materials.

The whole nature of man tends towards freedom; he therefore carries the proof in his own person that as *material* for the theatre he is useless. In the modern theatre, owing to the use of the bodies of men and women *as their material*, all which is presented there is of an accidental nature. The actions of the actor's body, the expression of his face, the sounds of his voice, all are at the mercy of the winds of his emotions: these winds, which must blow for ever round the artist, moving without unbalancing him. But with the actor, emotion *possesses* him; it seizes upon his limbs, moving them whither it will. He is at its beck and call, he moves as one in a frantic dream or as one distraught, swaying here and there; his head, his arms, his feet, if not utterly beyond control, are so weak to stand against the torrent of his passions, that they are ready to play him false at any moment. It is useless for him to attempt to reason with himself. Hamlet's calm directions (the dreamer's, not the logician's directions, by the way) are thrown to the winds. His limbs refuse, and refuse again to obey his mind the instant emotion warms, while the mind is all the time creating the heat which shall set these emotions afire. As with his movement, so is it with the expression of his face. The mind struggling and succeeding for a moment, in moving the eyes, or the muscles of the face whither it will; the mind bringing the face for a few moments into thorough subjection, is suddenly swept aside by the emotion which has grown hot through the action of the mind. Instantly, like lightning, and before the mind has time to cry out and protest, the hot passion has mastered the actor's expression. It shifts and changes, sways and turns, it is chased by emotion from the actor's forehead between his eyes and down to his mouth; now he is entirely at the mercy of emotion, and crying out to it: 'Do with me what you will!' His expression runs a mad riot hither and thither, and lo! 'Nothing is coming of nothing.' It is the same with his voice as it is with his movements. Emotion cracks the voice of the actor. It sways his voice to join in the conspiracy against his mind. Emotion works upon the voice of the actor, and he produces the impression of discordant emotion. It is of no avail to say that emotion is the spirit of the gods, and is precisely what the artist aims to produce; first of all this is not true, and even if it were quite true, every stray emotion, every casual feeling, cannot be of value. Therefore the mind of the actor, we see, is less powerful than his emotion, for emotion is able to win over the mind to assist in the destruction of that which the mind would produce; and as the mind becomes the slave of the emotion it follows that accident upon accident must be continually occurring. So then, we have arrived at this point: that emotion is the cause which first of all creates, and secondly destroys. Art, as we have said, can admit of no accidents. That, then, which the actor gives us, is not a work of art; it is a series of accidental confessions. In the beginning the human body was not used as material in the Art of the Theatre. In the beginning the emotions of men and women were not considered as a fit exhibition for the multitude. An elephant and a tiger in an arena suited the taste better, when the desire was to excite.

... the body of man ... is *by nature* utterly useless as a material for an art. I am fully aware of the sweeping character of this statement; and as it concerns men and women who are alive, and who as a class are ever to be loved, more must be said lest I give unintentional offence. I know perfectly well that what I have said here is not yet going to create an exodus of all the actors from all the theatres in the world, driving them into sad monasteries where they will laugh out the rest of their lives, with the Art of the Theatre as the main topic for amusing conversation. As I have written elsewhere, the theatre will continue its growth and actors will continue for some years to hinder its development. But I see a loophole by which in time the actors can escape from the bondage they are in. They must create for themselves a new form of acting, consisting for the main part of symbolical gesture. Today they *impersonate* and interpret; tomorrow they must *represent* and interpret; and the third day they must create. By this means style may return. Today the actor impersonates a certain being. He cries to the audience: 'Watch me; I am now pretending to be so and so, and I am now pretending to do so and so;' and then he proceeds to *imitate* as exactly as possibly, that which he has announced he will *indicate*. For instance, he is Romeo. He tells the audience that he is in love, and he proceeds to show it, by kissing Juliet. This, it is claimed, is a work of art: it is claimed for this that it is an intelligent way of suggesting thought. Why – why, that is just as if a painter were to draw upon the wall a picture of an animal with long ears and then write under it 'This is a donkey.' The long ears made it plain enough, one would think, without the inscription, and any child of ten does as much. The difference between the child of ten and the artist is that the artist is he who by drawing certain signs and shapes creates the impression of a donkey: and the greater artist is he who creates the impression of the whole genus of donkey, the *spirit* of the thing.

The actor looks upon life as a photo-machine looks upon life; and he attempts to make a picture to rival a photograph. He never dreams of his art as being an art such for instance as music. He tries to reproduce

Nature; he seldom thinks to invent with the aid of Nature, and he never dreams of *creating*. As I have said, the best he can do when he wants to catch and convey the poetry of a kiss, the heat of a fight, or the calm of death, is to copy slavishly, photographically – he kisses – he fights – he lies back and mimics death – and, when you think of it, is not all this dreadfully stupid? Is it not a poor art and a poor cleverness, which cannot convey the spirit and essence of an idea to an audience, but he can only show an artless copy, a facsimile of the thing itself? This is to be an imitator, not an artist. This is to claim kinship with the ventriloquist.

There is a stage expression of the actor 'getting under the skin of the part'. A better one would be getting '*out* of the skin of the part altogether'. 'What, then,' cries the red-blooded and flashing actor, 'is there to be no flesh and blood in this same art of the theatre of yours? No life?' It depends what you call life, signor, when you use the word in relation with the idea of art. The painter means something rather different to actuality when he speaks of life in his art, and the other artists generally mean something essentially spiritual; it is only the actor, the ventriloquist, or the animal-stuffer who, when they speak of putting life into their work, mean some actual and lifelike reproduction, something blatant in its appeal, that it is for this reason I say that it would be better if the actor should get out of the skin of the part altogether. If there is any actor who is reading this, is there not some way by which I can make him realise the preposterous absurdity of this delusion of his, this belief that he should aim to make an actual copy, a reproduction?

. . . I am not sure I do not wish that photography had been discovered before painting, so that we of this generation might have had the intense joy of advancing, showing that photography was pretty well in its way, but there was something better!' 'Do you hold that our work is on a level with photography?' 'No, indeed, it is not half as exact. It is less of an art even than photography. . . .

Eleanora Duse has said: 'To save the theatre, the theatre must be destroyed, the actors and actresses must all die of the plague. They poison the air, they make art impossible.'

We may believe her. . . . The actor must go, and in his place comes the inanimate figure – the Über-marionette we may call him, until he has won for himself a better name. Much has been written about the puppet, or marionette. There are some excellent volumes upon him, and he has also inspired several works of art. Today in his least happy period many people come to regard him as rather a superior doll – and to think he has developed from the doll. This is incorrect. He is a descendant of the stone images of the old temples – he is today a rather degenerate form of a god. Always the close friend of children, he still knows how to select and attract his devotees.

When any one designs a puppet on paper, he draws a stiff and comic-looking thing. Such an one has not even perceived what is contained in the idea which we now call the marionette. He mistakes gravity of face and calmness of body for blank stupidity and angular deformity. Yet even modern puppets are extraordinary things. The applause may thunder or dribble, their hearts beat no faster, no slower, their signals do not grow hurried or confused; and, though drenched in a torrent of bouquets and love, the face of the leading lady remains as solemn, as beautiful and as remote as ever. There is something more than a flash of genius in the marionette, and there is something in him more than the flashiness of displayed personality. The marionette appears to me to be the last echo of some noble and beautiful art of a past civilisation. But as with all art which has passed into fat or vulgar hands, the puppet has become a reproach. All puppets are now but low comedians.

They imitate the comedians of the larger and fuller blooded stage. They enter only to fall on their back. They drink only to reel, and make love only to raise a laugh. They have forgotten the counsel of their mother the Sphinx. Their bodies have lost grave grace, they have become stiff. Their eyes have lost that infinite subtlety of seeming to see; now they only stare. They display and jingle their wires and are cock-sure in their wooden wisdom. They have failed to remember that their art should carry on it the same stamp of reserve that we see at times on the work of other artists, and that the highest art is that which conceals the craft and forgets the craftsman. . . .

May we not look forward with hope to that day which shall bring back to us once more the figure, or symbolic creature, made also by the cunning of the artist, so that we can gain once more the 'noble artificiality' which the old writer speaks of? Then shall we no longer be under the cruel influence of the emotional confessions of weakness which are nightly witnessed by the people and which in their turn create in the beholders the very weaknesses which are exhibited. To that end we must study to remake these images – no longer content with a puppet, we must create an Über-marionette. The Über-marionette will not compete with life – rather will it go beyond it. Its ideal will not be the flesh and blood but rather the body in trance – it will aim to clothe itself with a death-like beauty while exhaling a living spirit. Several times in the course of this essay has a word or two about Death found its way on to the paper – called there by the incessant clamouring of 'Life! Life! Life!' which the realists keep up. And this might be easily mistaken for an affectation, especially by those who have no sympathy or delight in the power and the mysterious joyousness which is in all passionless works of art. . . .

To speak of a puppet with most men and women is to cause them to giggle. They think at once of the wires; they think of the stiff hands and the jerky movements; they tell me it is 'a funny little doll'. But let me tell them a few things about these puppets. Let me again repeat that they are the descendants of a great and noble family of images, images which were indeed made 'in the likeness of God'; and that many centuries ago these figures had a rhythmical movement and not a jerky one; had no need for wires to support them, nor did they speak through the nose of the hidden manipulator. . . . I pray earnestly for the return of the image – the Über-marionette to the theatre; and when he comes again and is but seen, he will be loved so well that once more will it be possible for the people to return to their ancient joy in ceremonies – once more will Creation be celebrated – homage rendered to existence – and divine and happy intercession made to Death.

from *A Durable Theatre* (1921)

PERFORMERS

And the performers? What of the actors, as they are called, and very well called? Do not fear that I am going to spring an Über-marionette into the midst of them. If he arrives it will be no case of my bringing him there, but because no one can prevent him from coming. I have no desire to thrust forward an unwelcome monster such as Frankenstein created into the midst of such durable and precious things as we have already arranged for. It is likely that the drama of which I have spoken will demand the services of man as performer; I have been told (since I wrote of the Über-marionette) of a race of actors that existed (and a few today preserve the tradition) who were fitted to be part of the most durable theatre it is possible to conceive. When I heard of this I was astounded, pleasurably astounded. I was told that this race of actors was so noble, sparing themselves no pain and austerely disciplining themselves, that all the weaknesses of the flesh were eradicated, and nothing remained but the perfect man. This race was not English or American, but Indian.

I am not sceptical. I would sooner be proved wrong in all my beliefs and theories than think man unable to rise to any standard known or to be known.

And so I accept this information, new though it be to me, and will present it here as a possibility; I will hope for it, even with my eyes and ears amazed at what they see and hear coming from the Western actors.

If the Western actor can become what I am told the Eastern actor was and is, I withdraw all that I have written in my essay, 'On the Actor and the Über-marionette.'

Strange that this Eastern land, so believing in the power of man to become divine, should make so many idols – so many beautiful idols – for idols are Über-marionettes.

In the event of man being unable to return to that ancient standard of the East, there is nothing open for us but to fashion something to represent man in this creative and durable art that we are contemplating.

Stanislavsky's System (1937)

They who know Stanislavsky, know very well what a remarkable actor he is off the stage: and for this reason it is difficult to estimate how good he is as an actor on the stage.

I have seen him in a dozen of his performances, in all of which he has done as thorough good work as is to be found in any theatre in Europe. He never attempts to electrify the spectators, yet never disappoints them. Everything is thought out most carefully, conscientiously planned – but as he is lacking in that ancient and instinctive sense of measure which belongs to the dancer, he is apt to hesitate and to drag. Lacking, too, that light and intangible genius of Lemaître or a Giovanni Grasso, he is none the less an undeniable example of the valuable, good actor. The first time you see him on the stage, his earnestness may so capture you that you may overrate him as an actor. Later, you come to note the subtlety of this man who, while acting a part – itself a deception – doubles his effect by deceiving you into a belief that he has done more than he actually has done.

As stage director he is admirable, being a very patient and kindly teacher. He begs his students to trust him, and then he teaches them according to his system. Young men and women without much natural talent respond to his persuasive logic: yet over some of us there creeps the suspicion that here is a stage manager who is using the curious gift – possessed by the trainer of elephants and seals – creatures only to be trained by kindness – creatures who after a few years of training acquire a capacity to do clever tricks which seem more extraordinary than they actually are.

Stanislavsky has always been a searcher. He does not seek to discover a simple truth, for the obvious does not appeal to him. He prefers, when looking for the highroad, to turn his back to it, to enter into the forest and grope in the very thickest of the undergrowth. If asked why he has left the highroad he will reply that everyone knows *that* highroad, and he prefers to look for others. Briefly his tendency is to avoid the ordinary, plain truth, and to search for more unusual truths in unlikely directions.

It is unnecessary to devote years of a life to teaching would-be actors to be, above all things, 'natural', since drama at its best is supernatural or 'spiritual'.

The hundred most excellent plays of the world are supernatural in form and in content. The Indian, the Chinese, the Japanese, the Greek, the Shakespearean and the Spanish dramas are natural enough, but they hold the mirror well up.

It is therefore better that the actor should avoid *as far as possible* the attempt to interpret these plays in a 'natural' way.

Acting is not an art – acting is an act. The performance of a play is an experience shared with the spectators at a play. But it is a more than ordinary experience, for the soul carried by the actor is seen in an adventure, and the spectators go along with it. It is a serious, but a strange business.

There can be no drama if the soul, 'that very fiery particle', be excluded: all the same, a measure of the 'natural' is to be found in great drama, in acting and in *mise-en-scène*. Be it only pretty – artless – funny – foul – ugly or trivial, it has its uses. Equally absurd would it be to teach would-be actors to be unnatural.

To be *true-to-nature* or *false-to-nature* – it is not this which has to be learnt by would-be actors.

None but born actors should be trained to act.

A very little training helps the born-actor: nothing can help the would-be-actor who lacks the essence of acting in his composition.

There are comparatively few born-actors working in theatres today: the made-up article, pressed into service by the Stanislavskys and others eager to develop 'new talent', has led to the gradual retirement of genuine born-actors.

It is for all these reasons that I am opposed to the '*système Stanis-lavsky*' and to every other system, for they threaten genius and stifle expression, and open but a small path to 'new talent' which they manage to mechanise – and that is all.

These systems, invented by men of intelligence who seem to be destitute of vision, are drawn up with an eye.

> Firstly, to helping the beginner
> Secondly, to helping the grown actor
> and Thirdly, to making him realise
> the importance of what is called
> 'natural' acting.

These systems and their misleading textbooks are drawn up to rid the actor of 'artificiality' (something so akin to art that to destroy it is very dangerous) and to create in him that feeling which a born-actor is never without, and which cannot be pumped into anyone.

Do they achieve what they set out to do? Unfortunately yes, fortunately no. They do help the beginner, but he is generally one who ought never to be encouraged to go on the stage: they quite fail to create in him that sense which the born-actor always possesses. They do rid the actor of some of his artificiality: but at the same time they instil into him another kind of artificiality, inferior to the old one. And while they make him realise the importance of what is called 'natural' acting, they chase away all that is lyrical in him.

There was one born-actor in the Moscow Art Theatre: his name was Artem. This was the actor that Chekhov loved to watch even before he came into the Moscow Art Theatre. Stanislavsky mentions his name once or twice in his book *My Life in Art*, but does not tell us anything about him.

I will tell you a little. Artem's acting was like Charles Lamb's writing . . . whoever has read and enjoyed Lamb's essays or letters will understand what I mean. Artem all the time twinkled with fun, which shone out triumphantly against what appeared to be an incomprehensible sadness: and this twinkling constituted his 'play'. He had a marvellous little voice which played about, now like a flute, now like a penny whistle – 'naturally' enough, but with innumerable accents in it which were much more than merely 'natural'. His face accompanied his voice, always changing its expression – not like an ape, for it was the visualised spirit of a man, and his gestures were very few. No one could say that he disguised himself so that he might be taken for another person – he was all persons in his own person, so there was no need for any of those diguises so loved by second-class actors.

All he tried for, then, was to express himself through the thoughts and words of Chekhov which he could understand so very well. This he did with surpassing success. His coming on – his talk – his facial play and his exits, were all like a single piece of drifting music – or, as some say, 'like a poem'. Yes they were poems, or rather little verses of one small cycle of poems. He was the cycle itself; all he had to do (and that *all* was a life's work) was to come and go, to speak and pause – to mutter and chirrup – to smile and laugh a little. Then to stop speech, smile, laughing and all. Taking these up again, he would continue to laugh a little more, to move a very little, to say a word or two half-heard, and one maybe better heard – to turn to look and look again – and then again.

What character was he representing in this play – what in that? 'Oh . . .' and then 'really', he seemed to say – and 'after . . .' – an apologetic little sideways smile, his eyes squinnied up: and 'After all, you . . .' – twig the little catastrophe? . . . 'What? Are you there? – I see you. . . .' All he seemed to say, seemed made up of a hundred such half-formed thoughts and sentences . . . followed by a faint squeak – a blinking of his eyes. All final though. All as clever as clever can be – questions and apologetic answers thrown out, saying something good, and something young. This old man Artem (he had been a schoolmaster for years) had so well preserved the heart of his youth, keeping it to serve his craft, that he was never less than natural from the moment he came on to the stage to the moment he went off – if to be natural is to stop acting and to *be*.

'A perfect actor', said those who could discern: the others said nothing and saw nothing . . . and there is no greater achievement possible to an actor than to be able to prevent a number of fools even seeing or hearing him.

This born actor could not have played Hamlet or Macbeth, perhaps: but I think he could have read both plays to us better than anyone else in Russia. He has all that all the Russian actors are trying to be today – and yet none will ever be what he was.

I have lately seen the remarkable Jewish actor Mikhoels play Lear, surrounded by a collective (we call it a company) which was all of a piece. Artem is gone, and only Mikhoels and his collective can fill his place: for just as Artem's playing was a song, so is theirs a song. Artem's tune was an old Russian theme, and Mikhoels and company have a Yiddish one. Artem attempted less; Mikhoels more. Artem was less theatrical (I am allowing for once the word 'theatrical' to carry a cheap sense), Mikhoels is more theatrical (putting the most resplendent sense possible on the word).

And of this Artem, this teacher by example of the entire Moscow Art Theatre group, Stanislavsky can say nothing.

It is probable that Stanislavsky saw nothing – how, then can he speak of what he never saw? But it is just because he sees so very little, that he can make a text-book for would-be actors – I mean, men without a glimmer of *bon théâtre* in their composition – a book for excellent dummies who would like to be famous and who probably will be, without ever coming to act like true actors.

It's all much on a par with what is going on in other walks of life today, where we see politicians manufactured from men without any political instinct, yet climbing to high place: composers manufactured, lacking all sense of the musical, dead to all sense of rhythm, but fully purposed to write music: men who become painters without possessing a sense of form or of colour, or become novelists because they have read a book – one; or poets, having twice taken tea with a poetess. And there must be something strangely upside-down in the modern development of the individual, when we find men who are born poets, serving badly behind a bar, and others, born to be fine composers, employed as poor estate agents. And there are second-rate waiters with gifts for the church or literature; artisans on the railways who have a genuine gift as painters; priests who were born to be jockeys. And so it goes on: muddle from the day a boy gropes to be something, and no one informed enough, nor any committee with a plan practical enough to say what he was born to be and to keep him to that – help him at that – and hand him to the nation as a first-class unit.

And I thoroughly distrust this book by Stanislavsky, because he guarantees that he and his system can make a good actor out of any man, no matter what he was born to be.

And to you who work in the amateur theatre in England, I would say that you do well if your whole aim be *to discover and support the born actor*: but if you all push your little talents forward, and not his, you will fail in what I think the whole movement was planned for, and you will do your country a disservice, not a service.

from *To Feel or Not to Feel. The Old Old Question* (1924)

What purpose Mr Grein can possibly have for asking London actors to write down for *The Illustrated London News* their theories on the worn out, quite clear, but still vexing question of whether actors should feel or not feel we do not know. That the actors have written very well indeed on this subject, (dealt with by Diderot in 1773–1774), is not surprising; and if it helps Mr Grein to eke out his weekly page, 'The World of the Theatre' that is pleasant. But what they all say is only what Diderot told us all in the sixteenth century in his *Paradox of Acting* which we always remember with joy was quoted in the *Harms-*

worth Encyclopaedia as *The Paradise of Acting*. These slips will occur, thank heaven, and keep us merry.

But to return to the actors and Diderot's book and this deluding talk about whether an actor should feel murderous when pretending to murder another actor on the stage.

The truth is that it's like all other such questions, such as 'Should the stage be lighted by footlights or not?' The correct answer is 'some footlights'. 'How many?' cries the merciless accountant of art: the correct reply is 'as many as are necessary'.

Mr Casson and Miss Thorndike very properly mentioned the audience as being an essential part of the actor's work.

What Giovanni Grasso would have written about feeling a part we cannot imagine; but there again, if an English actor seems to feel very little and a southern actor very much, that's where the deception of nature is playing pranks with the deception of theatricals.

For a Chinese or Indian sage who sits like a bronze statue for four hours meditating, may be feeling more than either of these. He is feeling slower, that is all; forcing himself to the pace. And the English actor is slow too, the Italian quick. The Englishman is said to be calculating his effects, the Italian to be inspired. Recall Bonaparte's 'Inspiration is only a calculation made with rapidity.' 'Should an actor be slow or rapid?' one might ask this for a change. Irving was slow: Grasso was rapid. Why? because the blood and mind of the first were blood and mind of a curiously deliberate man. Is that bad for acting? Why should it be? The blood and brain of Grasso leapt with agility at all things. Is that bad for acting? Why should it be? But to be slow and be a bad actor, that is as bad for acting as to be rapidly bad.

In short, there is no actual formula, and never has been one. That is what Diderot seems to suggest so delightfully; so that Mr Grein's sententious air about it all is the only original touch.

from *The Art of the Theatre*. *The Second Dialogue* (1910)

STAGE DIRECTOR: When we have our scheme well supported – and £5,000 a year guaranteed for five years will be all we shall require – we shall put the following plan into action.

We shall build and equip a college, furnishing it with what is necessary.

It will have to contain two theatres, one open-air and one roofed-in. These two stages, closed and open, are necessary for our experiments and on one or on the other, sometimes on both, every theory shall be tested and records made of the results.

These records will be written, drawn, photographed or registered on the cinematograph or gramophone for future reference, but they will not be made public and will be only for the use of members of the college.

Other instruments for the study of natural sound and light will be purchased, together with the instruments for producing these artificially, and will lead us to the better knowledge of both sound and light, and also to the invention of yet better instruments through which the purer beauty of both sound and light may be passed.

In addition, instruments will be purchased for the study of motion, and some will be especially invented for this purpose.

To this equipment we shall add a printing-press, all kinds of carpenters' tools, a well-stocked library, and all things pertaining to modern theatres. With these materials and instruments we shall pursue the study of the stage as it is today with the intention of finding out those weaknesses which have brought it to its present unfortunate condition. We shall, in short, experiment upon the body of the modern theatre in our roofed-in theatre (for you will remember we have two), exactly in the same way as surgeons and their pupils experiment upon the bodies of dead men and animals.

In selecting its method of administration the college will follow the ancient precedent of nature. It will consist of a head, a body and its members, the leader being selected by election. Those who are to compose the executive body are less difficult to decide on, as their task is undoubtedly less difficult.

In all there will not be more than thirty men in the college. There will be no women.

So now, are you clear as to these two points? First, that we shall have a college of experiment in which to study the three natural sources of art – sound, light and motion – or, as I have spoken of them elsewhere, *voice, scene* and *action.*

Secondly, that we shall number in all thirty working-men, who shall singly and together pursue the study of the three subjects named and the other experiments to test the principles of the modern theatre.

from *Thoroughness in the Theatre* (1911)

THE SCHOOL

In talking about a school of experiment for an art such as the one I propose now, it will be best to avoid technical details as much as possible. How little illuminating would be a long description of the means

we shall employ in our experiments with light and the scene! How little
it would say to you if I described what we shall practise with the voice!
And how little you would be moved if I were to tell you how we are to
study the movements of nature!

All this would be more or less asking you to fix your attention upon
some dry book, or plan, or chart. Instead of that, let us walk through
the school. By seeing something of it you will understand far better.

Let us imagine that we are standing in the central hall of the building;
you look up, and seem surprised at the loftiness of it, with light coming
in from high windows. Already you do not feel as if you were in a
school. You ask what use is made of this room, and I point to one end
of it. There you see a large stage upon which the masters and assistants
are trying experiments with a new apparatus which we made last week,
for the purpose of casting a series of parallel shafts of light, each of
which has parallel edges – a most difficult yet a most desirable thing
to do, I assure you.

'But why are all those figures dressed in white, and why is the scene
white?'

'Well, we are interested for the moment in seeing how much colour
is to be found in the use of white light upon white objects.'

'And do you find any?'

'Oh, yes, quite a little.'

'I like a lot of colour. I saw such a blaze of colour when the Russian
Ballet came here. Do you not like the Russian Ballet and their stage
setting?'

'Yes, quite well. But to give you that we should need to make no
experiments. We should only have to buy some colours and then ask a
number of studio painters to give us a few months of their valuable
time to do our work for us. That is not exactly what we purpose doing
here. The whole reason of this school is that we may train *the men of
the theatre* to be able to do their own work for themselves – not to call
in the outsider. It seems to me rather a reasonable proposition, and it
seems to me utterly unreasonable for a serious institution like the theatre
to seem obliged to call in outsiders, however talented they may be, in
order to help us out of our difficulties. *What the stage has never yet
learned to do, is to surmount its own difficulties.*

'*I want to see the theatre entirely self-dependent. As it is, when it wants
colour, designs, costumes and lighting effects, it goes to artists who know
nothing about the theatre, they having practised the art of painting, which
is a totally different art.*

'I do not believe that I am the only person in the theatre who thinks like this. And, therefore, I believe that this school, when it opens and gets to work, will be very often visited by our theatrical friends.'

'Oh. I like *that*!'

This exclamation is caused by my visitor suddenly being carried away by something she sees upon the stage. She claps her hands, and says she 'has never seen anything so lovely before'.

'I am so pleased. That is the second reason why we made this school. *It was to give you and every one else all sorts of things that you had never seen before, and to give you pleasure through them.*'

'Yes, but it is wonderful! All that light pouring up like a torrent in great waves. How exciting!'

'Yes. That is the third reason; to excite you. Why, the school seems to be quite a success in the first five minutes!'

'Yes, but tell me what is that experiment for?'

'You mean, what play is it for?'

'Yes.'

'It is *for* no particular play. It is for the sake of the experiment; it is in order to find out, and know more than others. And we come across such things every day when making our experiments.'

'Yes, but can't you put it to some use, so that every one can see it?'

'Do you think people would like to see it?'

'Why, there is nobody who would not be excited if they saw such a thing as that upon the stage.'

'Well, then, perhaps sooner or later we shall find some manager who will want such things – some manager who wants to excite his audience. After all, exciting impressions in a theatre are rare enough nowadays, but one must not force them on to the stage or they are out of place.'

'Now do tell me how you discover things like that!'

'The reason is that we have *time* in which to discover them. That is the first requisite. Then we have the place. That is the second. Then we have the idea. That is the third. Then, with unlimited material to use, we merely work away until we find it out. If we had to try and create any such impression in a theatre we should not be able to do so, because we have not the time there to devote to such a search, nor the material, and because we have to produce plays by, let us say, March 1st or July 5th, at a given hour, and we are under contract to do so.'

'But are there not workshops in London, Rome and Paris where they have time, and where their whole year's work consists in making experiments in their own branches? Are there not theatrical electricians, theatrical scene painters, theatrical costumiers, and do they do nothing?'

'Oh, certainly; they do wonders. These suppliers of "effects" to the

theatres are possibly the most capable of men. The scene painters are
undoubtedly the most admirable scene painters, and what costumiers
we have! And the electricians are first-class.

'But it is valueless to consider all these things *separately*, or of separate
people supplying them to the theatres, since they have to be judged as a
whole when united? You may paint the most perfect scene in the world,
and you may bring in the most perfect lighting apparatus in the theatre,
but, *unless the two things, together with the actor and the actor's voice*,
have been considered as a unit, the most dire results must always be
produced. . . .'

'But what about the study of acting?'

'My dear madam, do you suppose that we should attempt to teach
that which every one has told us is unteachable? Miss Ellen Terry has
said that acting is not to be taught, and many others have said so too,
and we are entirely of their opinion. It cannot be taught.

'But what *can* be taught is this; how to walk from one side of the
stage to the other; but that is moving – that is not acting. You can be
taught how to move arms, legs, and torso with expression; that is not
acting – that again is moving. You can be taught how to move your
face; you can even be taught how to move your soul – or rather, how to
allow your soul to move you – but this is still not acting. That comes
under the head of movement. Then you can be taught how to produce
your voice so that it reaches to every part of the building and into the
soul of the listener. You can be taught how not to speak; but all this is
not acting, it is speaking.

'In fact, this school does not attempt to teach as you teach parrots. It
attempts to give men the necessary equipment to produce a play from
first to last. I have, for instance, designed scenes all my life, but I have
never been *taught* that. But I remember well there was a time in my life
when I would have given much if I could have been shown how to do
that which should lead to the producing of a play, that which should
lead to the designing of scenes and that which should lead to the acting
of a part.

'It is just for this reason that I call this a "school of experiment".
When you experiment, you find out for yourself. At any other school
you become like a parrot, and you imitate. The faculty for imitation is
not what I want my school to develop – it is to develop the creative
faculty. If you study how to copy accounts, how to write shorthand,
how to make bricks, or any other work requiring diligent application
only, you can be taught by careful directors; but if you attempt to teach
even so delicate an art as that of cooking, neither careful direction nor

diligent application will achieve anything more than technical perfection.

'This idea nowadays that all tasks undertaken can be likened to one another leads to confusion in the minds of workers in every branch. Let us divide them now. There are workers with the hands, workers with the head, and workers with the soul; and the qualities of these three tasks are as separate as are the earth, the sea and the sky from one another. That which your hand learns, you can be taught; that which your head learns, you can only teach yourself; and that which your soul learns, is God-sent.

'This school is to teach that which the hand can learn, and to experiment with the hand; it is also to make it possible for us to teach ourselves those things which the head can learn; and if we happen to have among our members one or more of those elect people whom the gods have taken thought to teach, then so much the better.

'We may by good fortune do inspired work – but good or ill fortune, the day we have our workshops or "school" all our work shall be *thorough*.'

On Learning Magic (1921)

A DIALOGUE MANY TIMES REPEATED
> '*The most foolish error of all is made by clever young men in thinking that they forfeit their originality if they recognise a truth which has already been recognised by others.*' . . . Goethe

PUPIL: I want to join your school and to study the Art of the Theatre.

MASTER: Let me do my best to point out to you the hardships connected with the study of the Art.

You have to give up every other study and think only of this one.

You have to begin from the beginning.

You have to come to me knowing nothing, and, what is more, realising that you know nothing.

You have to feel discontented with yourself and not with me.

You have to be prepared to work ten to fifteen years at the craft.

You have to realise that before you can create a drama you must be able to speak so as to be heard, to walk across a room or a stage with ease, to have studied the movements of marionettes for many years, to love nature better than your own self, to know the whole history of the drama from its earliest days, to absorb all theories, be able to do humblest services – and be an honest man.

PUPIL: Oh, I can do all this easily. I love the idea so much, and you are such a wonderful man.

MASTER: That has nothing to do with it, and all depends on you. Do you know what is a stage rostrum?

PUPIL: I suppose it is a raised pulpit of some kind.

MASTER: It is a raised stage of wood, composed of a collapsible framework and a movable top. (*The* MASTER *here draws a plan of this.*) It is used in modern theatres to build up the scene with. Thus at the far end of a flight of steps we shall place a rostrum so that it may act as a landing place. Do you understand?

PUPIL: Oh, yes, of course!

MASTER: I am glad you find that easy to grasp. In *Julius Caesar* at His Majesty's Theatre, in *Faust* at the Lyceum, and in *Tannhauser* at Bayreuth many such rostrums were used.

PUPIL: But why do you tell me all this?

MASTER: Do you know what is a stage brace?

PUPIL: No, but what has that to do with the Art of the Theatre as hinted at in your book?

MASTER: A stage brace is a wooden support, adjustable to any reasonable height, and used in the modern theatre to prop up pieces of stage scenery which are neither hung nor self-supporting. (*He draws a plan of the stage brace.*) Do you know what 'properties' are?

PUPIL: But I want to study Art with you, not tricks.

MASTER: A great poet has told us that all Art is a trick; therefore do not despise tricks. You say you want to study Art – and you begin by despising the humblest parts of the Art.

PUPIL: But rostrums and braces and properties are things which children of ten or twelve years old might learn about and profit by knowing.

MASTER: Whereas you are a superior person and wish to learn the Art? Let me tell you that you will never learn the Art until you are modest enough to desire to learn all about the humblest parts of the structure of theatres – scenery, costumes, and acting – and to learn it thoroughly. Do you really suppose that the carrying of a banner is an easy matter? Do you really believe you are so gifted a person that you can afford to skip the experience of saying, 'My lord, the carriage waits'?

PUPIL: But, master, I thought you hated all that nonsense. I thought you detested Bayreuth, the Lyceum, and His Majesty's. I thought you wrote and fought against all the old-fashioned stage for years – that you planned out a new stage which you believed in, and which was to be the stage of the future.

MASTER: You see how far wrong you are in your reading of my thoughts. I have planned out a new stage, certainly; but not because I despise or hated the old stage – because I love it, and lived near it many years.

And though I may wish to create a new stage, I know the old one; and to know it is to love, even if one does not agree with it. I worked in the old theatre for more than ten years before I began to construct the new.

You wish to begin where I left off. Such vanity, such shifting of responsibilities, is no use to you.

You say you want to come to my school.

I tell you you had better keep away unless you realise that you have firstly *no right* to despise the old stage, and secondly *no chance* of practising the new Art until you have paid the very humblest tribute to the old institution, by studying all those things which at present you dare to despise.

You came here expecting me to tear up the old theatre before your eyes. You expected to find an accomplice, and you are surprised to find a master.

When you read in my book that I was all on the side of the young men and against the managers, you thought that you would plot with me to blow them to the moon. But on coming here you hear me speaking well of the managers and advocating a thorough study of their methods. That makes you mad. And you will never be able to understand my reasons for being balanced.

I quarrelled with the managers and the conditions of the stage only after having studied the theatre for over twelve years – but I quarrelled openly. I have no wish to be a conspirator.

A conspirator is a sneak. This school is not to produce sneaks.

Here with me you learn first to love the old theatre. I hand on to you what my old master taught me, and I will tell you where I think he may have erred, but I do not want your understanding to become thick and muddy by drunkenly jeering at his errors. The 'errors' were far better than all your 'virtues'. And you will only advance and do well if you are honest, modest, and open-minded.

PUPIL: I think I have changed my opinion – and I do not wish to come to your school; for I am not a baby and will learn to be honest and modest somewhere else.

(*He goes out, and the master proceeds with his work, firmly convinced that the real pupil with character is never far off.*)

from *A Letter to Ellen Terry* (1917)

What is the last word? What is all this driving at, do you think?

The Liberation of the Actor.

Have I suggested too little for him? Will it all be too fragmentary? Would he rather have us demand from him a perfect, a completed work of art in the first years of his trial? How can a child be asked to race like a man, or even to walk like a youth?

Always, and now here, again, *I ask only for the liberation of the actor that he may develop his own powers*, and cease from being the marionette of the playwright.

4. Stage Visions

The artistic independence of the director in the twentieth century has made it possible for a production to take on a personal stamp other than that of the playwright or the leading actor. From this independence was born a new form of the theatre of the dominant idea, in which the various of emphases possible within the performances of all the characters were examined and the external factors, period, setting, costume, stage effects were coordinated by the director to produce a unity. In this unity could be discerned the single guiding hand whose task combined both the inspiration and the means by which it could be realised.

The new power won for the director led to all kinds of excess. Perhaps it still does, though whatever vogues may come and go, the director is surely here to stay. Stanislavsky's embellishment of the plays of Chekhov with effects and business is notorious, and the compulsive adorning of the Moscow Art Theatre's *Julius Caesar* with realistic detail of old Rome bordered on the manic: but Stanislavsky was always ready to learn from experience. Reinhardt and Meyerhold were less pliable, equating a personal view with personal tyranny. Craig too must be regarded as having overstated the case for the 'Über-director', at least in the light of modern practice, but the director as creator has flourished, and Craig deserves some credit for promoting him.

Much of this promotion resided not so much in Craig's reassessment of plays as in what he chose to call 'stage visions'. In a whole series of engravings, drawings and models he created his own 'new theatre', combining his graphic gifts with a massive instinct for a theatre of tableau.

Many of his designs from all periods of his working life were not settings devised for a production on which he was engaged. They were illustrations of ideas, some of stage directions, some of contrasts in background and light, some of pure emotion or arrested movement, some of the flexibility of a geometric stage geography. To the receptive they can propose all the power of the moments in the theatre which audiences remember, those moments which make the scalp tingle and the heart miss a beat.

Considered as mere designs they give ammunition to those who dismiss Craig's ideas as the excesses of the talented amateur: but they are not simply designs. The four moods of 'The Steps' were not intended to be a setting for any play. They are guides to all theatre practitioners as to how contrast and shadow set up an association in the mind. They amplify Craig's belief in the sculptural quality of the physical actor, in whom posture relates to the other actors and the background to promote a dominant feeling. They advertise, as words sometimes fail to do, how Craig advocated a total stage picture with a painter's eye and a director's intuition.

He worked on the ideas of *Scene* for many years. Much of his early work was notable for the way in which it promoted verticals. The eye is constantly carried forwards and upwards by enormous arches, by cliffs, by towering walls. It was this as much as anything which led to the accusations of impracticality when it became apparent that the scale of the human figure to the background appeared to recommend settings of upwards of sixty feet in height. Critics tore into these ideas as though Craig has somehow blundered over his sums, instead of seeing that the plans were not plans but illustrations of perspectives and priorities. Among the variety of work which went to make up *Scene* he attempted to come to terms with actual practice by constructing a single working setting whose variety would be inexhaustible. *The Thousand Scenes in One Scene* describes it and reveals a canniness about practical matters which should disarm the hardiest opponent.

The exhibition held at the Victoria and Albert Museum in 1967 included one particularly striking contrast. On one wall was one of Craig's *Hamlet* illustrations, not a design for the Moscow production but a 'vision'. The etching is no more than six inches by four but it was blown up in a photograph to cover a whole wall from floor to ceiling. The human figure was still no more than fourteen inches high. On the opposite side of the room was a model of a set of screens and levels which revolved slowly (though not slowly enough) throwing contrasting areas into highlight and silhouette from a fixed and simple light source. The model could have been no more than two feet high at most, but it served as an admirable reminder that in whatever other ways Craig may have been an impractical man, it was nothing to do with a defective 'eye'.

Scene was the outcome of a search for complete flexibility of floor-space, surround and backing, 'a room or place moveable at all parts'.

The movement of background screens during the action of a play inspired the setting for *Hamlet* at the Moscow Arts Theatre, the infamous example of when the practice of the theatre proved unequal to the idea. Screens were used successfully by Yeats in Dublin, based on Craig's drawings, and work in and around their use was continued until the publication of *Scene* in 1923. Edward Craig's reaction is vivid and revealing:

'Following the publication of *Scene* in the summer of 1923, I came to know for the first time what his etchings represented; until then, I, like so many others, had presumed that they were various scenes from an imaginary drama. As soon as I realised that each etching was a piece of arrested action within a great symphony of movement, I longed to see the progression of this movement in three dimensions. Father said tersely, "We'll get to that one day . . . later."'

His son then relates the explosion when he admitted that he had asked a hydraulics expert for advice on how to make the model work. Craig, clearly a sick man at the time, accused Edward of treachery and betrayal. The model he hid in a cellar. It was not seen again.

Edward, now, is quite sure that of all his father's work, the ideas for *Scene* have most to offer as an inspiration to contemporary designers and directors.

Enter the Army (1900)

That's a stage direction, and *that*'s a drama.

I sometimes live in Trafalgar Square, where all sorts of undramatic things go on all day long, but when I hear a band in the distance, and I see the troops coming along, I feel that although it is merely a regiment of men, it is dramatic. What you may say is, that it is theatrical. Strange, that troops marching so trimly should be called theatrical! That the army may be General Booth's army, and that they are carrying his coffin to the grave, does not seem to me to make it more dramatic, but the fact that it is a body of men in uniform and that it is marching in unison, *that* seems to me very dramatic. If they were all divided and split up, in what way would they differ from the ordinary? In the entrance of the army we return to the old feeling that was in the entrance of the chorus in the Greek drama or the entrance of the choir in the medieval drama. The idea of the chorus may be old-fashioned to some people. Certainly the spirit of harmony and uniformity is not a very modern spirit, and, except in the army, or among the police, or in a cricket match, we seldom are aware of its presence. But in art, it seems to me entirely forgotten, and yet it is the one essential thing that should be remembered.

Well – 'exit the army'.

The Arrival (1901)

This is for no particular play, but it is for what I believe to be true drama.

The name explains the drama. The first picture in this volume ('Enter the Army') is a stage direction; so is 'The Arrival' a kind of stage direction. It tells us of something which is being done, and not of something which is being said, and the fact that we do not know who is arriving and why they are arriving, or what they will look like when they appear, makes it, to my mind, dramatic. 'And,' you will say, 'unsatisfying'. That depends. That depends if you are more interested in the end than in the middle or the beginning. It seems to me that the longer one postpones the end, the more exciting life must be. To open the golden doors and find nothing but great glittering stars, to have to admit to Bill 'that there ain't no heaven', seems to me a stupid thing to hasten. Provided that you do not open the doors, you never know, and that is heaven. Maeterlinck, of course, maintains that to know the room one sits in is to find it heaven, but that won't do.

I feel that dramas should never tell you anything. I don't mean that you should never hear any words spoken, although that would be a great blessing, but the things done, the ambitions awakened, should never be finished – they should always be a mystery; and mystery no longer exists the moment things finish; mystery dies when you touch the soul of things or see the soul quite clearly. Then, what nonsense we talk when we speak about the mystery of this play or that play, when these plays are perhaps rather mysterious, but entirely comprehensible. You wish that I would be a little more comprehensible. If I wished to be, I should say what I said ten years ago, 'Give me a theatre', and then you shall be like blind Gloucester, and 'see feelingly'.

LEAR. Read.
GLOUCESTER. What, with this case of eyes?
LEAR. Oh, ho, are you there with me? No eyes in your head, nor no money in your purse? Your eyes are in a heavy case, your purse in a light; yet you see how this world goes.
GLOUCESTER. I see it feelingly.

But I no longer want a theatre. We no longer need theatres. We need first to become masters of the art. Let us turn, then, to our studies with all the seriousness left in us after hundreds of years 'pretending'.

The Steps *1* (1905)

FIRST MOOD

I think it is Maeterlinck who pointed out to us that drama is not only that part of life which is concerned with the good and bad feelings of individuals, and that there is much drama in life without the assistance of murder, jealousy, and the other first passions. He then leads us up to a fountain or into a wood, or brings a stream upon us, makes a cock crow, and shows us how dramatic these things are. Of course, Shakespeare showed us all that a few centuries earlier, but there is much good and no harm in having repeated it. Still I think that he might have told us that there are two kinds of drama, and that they are very sharply divided. These two I would call the drama of speech and the drama of silence, and I think that his trees, his fountains, his streams, and the rest come under the heading of the drama of silence – that is to say, dramas where speech becomes paltry and inadequate. Very well, then, if we pursue this thought further, we find that there are many things other than works of nature which enter into this drama of silence, and a very grand note in this drama is struck by that noblest of all men's work, architecture. There is something so human and so poignant to me in a great city at a time of the night when there are no people about and no sounds. It is dreadfully sad until you walk till six o'clock in the morning. Then it is very exciting. And among all the dreams that the architect has laid upon the earth, I know of no more lovely things than his flights of steps leading up and leading down, and of this feeling about architecture in my art I have often thought how one could give life (not a voice) to these places, using them to a dramatic end. When this desire came to me I was continually designing dramas wherein the place was architectural and lent itself to my desire. And so I began with a drama called 'The Steps'.

This is the first design, and there are three others. In each design, I show the same place, but the people who are cradled in it belong to each of its different moods. In the first it is light and gay, and three children are playing on it as you see the birds do on the back of a large hippopotamus lying asleep in an African river. What the children do I cannot tell you, although I have it written down somewhere. It is simply technical, and until seen it is valueless. But if you can hear in your mind's ear the little stamping sound which rabbits make, and can hear a rustle of tiny silver bells, you will have a glimpse of what I mean, and will be able to picture to yourself the queer quick little movements. Now on to the next one.

The Steps 2 (1905)

SECOND MOOD
You see that the steps have not changed, but they are, as it were, going to sleep, and at the very top of a flat and deep terrace we see many girls and boys jumping about like fireflies. And in the foregound, and farthest from them, I have made the earth respond to their movements.

The earth is made to dance.

The Steps 3 (1905)

THIRD MOOD

Something a little older has come upon the steps. It is very late evening
with them. The movement commences with the passing of a single
figure – a man. He begins to trace his way through the maze which is
defined upon the floor. He fails to reach the centre. Another figure
appears at the top of the steps – a woman. He moves no longer, and she
descends the steps slowly to join him. It does not seem to me very clear
whether she ever does join him, but when designing it I had hoped that
she might. Together they might once more commence to thread the
maze. But although the man and woman interest me to some extent, it
is the steps on which they move which move me. The figures dominate
the steps for a time, but the steps are for all time. I believe that some
day I shall get nearer to the secret of these things, and I may tell you
that it is very exciting approaching such mysteries. If they were dead,
how dull they would be, but they are trembling with a great life, more
so than that of man – than that of woman.

The Steps 4 (1905)

FOURTH MOOD

The steps this time have to bear more weight. It is full night, and to commence with, I want you to cover with your hand the carved marks on the floor and to shut out from your eyes the curved fountains at the top of the steps. Imagine also the figure which is leaning there, placed over on the other side of the steps – that is to say, in the shadow. He is heavy with some unnecessary sorrow, for sorrow is always unnecessary, and you see him moving hither and thither upon this highway of the world. Soon he passes on to the position in which I have placed him. When he arrives there, his head is sunk upon his breast, and he remains immobile.

Then things commence to stir; at first ever so slowly, and then with increasing rapidity. Up above him you see the crest of a fountain rising like the rising moon when it is heavy in autumn. It rises and rises, now and then in a great throe, but more often regularly. Then a second fountain appears. Together they pour out their natures in silence. When these streams have risen to their full height, the last movement commences. Upon the ground is outlined in warm light the carved shapes of two large windows, and in the centre of one of these is the shadow of a man and a woman. The figure on the steps raises his head. The drama is finished.

Study for Movement (1906)

Here we see a man battling through a snowstorm, the movements of both snow and man being made actual. Now I wonder whether it would be better if we should have no snowstorm visualised, but only the man, making his symbolical gestures which should suggest to us a man fighting against the elements. In a way I suppose this would be better. Still I have some doubts; for, following that line of argument in its logical sequence, then, would it not be still more near to art if we had no man, but only movements of some intangible material which would suggest the movements which the soul of man makes battling against the soul of nature? Perhaps it would be even better to have nothing at all. If this is to be, then art, being almost at its last gasp, today we seem to be nearer perfection than we were even in the days of the great symbolical designers of India. But if we are to have the actual man going through actual gestures, why not have the actual scene going through its actual pantomime?

I don't know if anybody is really interested in such questions; no one seems to be making any efforts to answer them one way or another. Let us turn over the page.

A Study for Movement (1906)

One can understand that people have something to do with movement, and that the moon has something to do with movement. What steps have to do with movement, except as the recipients of movers, is not as clear to me on one day as it is on another day, and here I feel inclined to speak right against these steps. The design has, I think, some feeling of movement in it, but when I come to think of the way some dancing school may probably plump a big flight of hard steps at the end of their room and make poor girls run up and down them, posing like the dreadful things we want to escape from, then I curse anything so material as steps in connection with movement, and regret that I ever made any record suggesting a connection between the two things.

A Palace, a Slum and a Stairway (1907)

I daresay that, looking at these and several of the other designs, you may imagine that in their original form they are grey, but they are not. For instance, this is a design in blue, yellow, white, red, and black. I mention this because grey is rather depressing, and to depress is not my wish.

I was asked how I should design a scene containing suggestions of the dwellings of the upper and lower classes, and also put into the scene a neutral spot where the two classes always met. So I designed, on the one side, a palace, of which the only thing palatial about it was its upright and severe form, and its golden colour, and on the other side slum, with its little windows and shadows, and its geranium in the window; and in between these two came a stairway, as the magic spot where the whole world meets practically in harmony. It is for no particular plot or play, but one can imagine that perhaps some day a writer or even a stage manager will perhaps plan a series of dramas dealing with these two classes, wherein we see them separated and then continually united. Who knows, I might do it with proper care myself if someone doesn't light-heartedly seize the idea carelessly and, slapping me on the back, tell me cheerily I'm good to steal from.

from *The Old School of Acting* (1915)

Towards the close of that first visit I asked him if there was time for him to look at some of my designs, and I spread these before him. They were a loose set of prints then on the eve of being issued in my book, *Towards a New Theatre*. He took them, and we began going through them, and every now and then he picked out certain designs and put them aside together in a heap. These designs which he had put aside he now took up and spread out before him. Then leaning back in his chair, he settled down and looked at them, saying a word which is more often used in Italy than elsewhere – '*bella*' – 'beautiful'.

His voice had again assumed the mysterious and hushed tones that he loved so much to play with on his stage, and of course I was very pleased.

But to receive praise was not my object in showing the designs to Salvin. I wanted to hear one thing from him, as the representative of the great days of acting, so I asked him, 'Will you please tell me, can the actor *act* in such a scene?'

He turned round as if the ghost in *Hamlet* was about to enter. He frowned, and said '*Macché!*' which is untranslatable, but means here, 'Why ask me such an amazing question?' and he added, 'These scenes *liberate* the actor; they liberate him from the little Gothic room in which he has been shut.' He then drew a big breath, spread out his chest, and put out his hands, as if about to address the Senate in that wonderful speech in *Othello*. – 'Most potent, grave, and reverend Signors': then he touched one of the steps in one of the designs. You felt he wanted to be moving on it.

I then told him that in England actors put forward the argument that, although the scenes were beautiful in themselves, they were impossible to be acted in.

His eyesbrows went up and down, he touched the design again and said in measured tones, 'The actor who cannot act in that scene is no true artist.' (*Non è artista.*)

from *Scene* (1923)

The scene stands by itself – and is monotone. All the colour used is produced by light, and I use a very great deal of colour now and again, – such colour as no palette ever can produce. I think I may say that I have not seen colour so rich used in any scene on any stage but this. . . .

Now for a word on this word 'simplified': . . . let me explain what I mean by it.

The world once used reed pens – then quill pens – and then steel pens. These they dipped into bottles of ink: many times would a man dip his pen into the ink before he could write a page of his letter.

Someone then invented the fountain pen. A man can write his whole letter without dipping his pen once into any bottle.

The world then invented the typewriting machine.

I would liken my scene to the fountain pen and not to the typewriting machine.

It is not a piece of mechanism; it is a simple device, shaped like screens – angular – plain.

Why is it shaped as it is? – why plain, flat screens or walls?

I will tell you. You must suppose me to be doing in front of you rapidly what it took me many years to do slowly. Suppose me, then, searching to find the essential form of the habitation of man, so as to afterwards making a stage habitation for the stage man.

I make rapidly two hundred and fifty models of his various habitations all over the earth. I make two as used by him 5000 B.C., three

2000 B.C., five 500 B.C., ten 100 B.C., twenty 100 A.D., thirty 1000 A.D., sixty 1500 A.D., fifty 1700 A.D., and seventy 1900 A.D.

I put them up in a line: – I study them.

I intend to reject every piece of each habitation which I do not find in all the others.

Why?

In order to discover which pieces every man since the year one has found essential.

Why?

So as to make *one* scene.

Why?

Because this scene-making is something of an art and not a toy factory.

I do not want the litter of the nursery in my theatre.

I do not want to waste yearly thousands of pounds on the usual bric-à-brac found in the modern theatre.

Because it is a waste of money – wood – canvas, and I do not want to waste the spectator's powers and temper as spectator and the artist's powers as artist. The artist is to speak to spectators through scene, he is not to display a large doll's house for them.

Having rejected in the two hundred and fifty models any piece which cannot be found in every other piece, I find I am then left with the essential parts which form the habitation of man. The walls remain:

The floor.

The ceiling . . . nothing else.

And how are these shaped?

Are there pillars on them, near them? – do parts protrude – the roof, for example? – some cornice – some skirting? Are there doors, windows, kerbs, and so forth? No. Because I found no such things in all the models. I found that the only things in every habitation of man were flat floor – flat walls – flat roof.

The flat roof is the only part of the human habitation which began at once to vary.

So now you see how it is that my screens, my SCENE, is composed as it is of plain flat walls. I wished to reduce scene to its essentials and I found it reduced itself. I have but done as ordered.

I then added mobility to it.

Why?

First because it seemed to demand it. Secondly because it continued to demand it. It demanded it on behalf of the actor. This mobility allows him to move in a differently shaped scene each night for as long as he wishes. Suppose he does not feel at home in this shape, he can change it and rechange it. It is like a hundred pairs of gloves – he can soon find a pair to fit and please him.

Being a device and not an actual habitation, it seemed to ask that I should so make it that it could *seem* now to be the inside and now the outside of any habitation ever known in the world – mud hut or temple, – Palais de Versailles or Mr Harrod's shop.

And can it be these four places?

It can *seem* like all four . . . it can seem like four hundred other places. It has a quite clear resemblance to four hundred different places.

I do not mean to say that I shall always show you the wallpaper that is in Mr Harrod's office . . . or always the gilding in Versailles Palace – or always the marble in the temple or the mud in the hut . . . But I will give you the form of the four places, the light belonging to each – and three or four details – here a door added – here a grille and here an alcove which, when you see them, shall somehow bring up to your mind the conviction that you see what I intend you to see.

And suppose I don't see what you intend me to see? you ask.

There will be thirty out of eighty who do not see as the other fifty see: – that I cannot help . . . that has always been so.

Some people going to see Irving as Mathias in *The Bells*, or Coquelin as M. Jourdain, saw Mathias and saw M. Jourdain. Some fewer number of people did not see any such thing; – they merely saw M. Coquelin and Irving. But if, like every real good playgoer, you go to the theatre to see what we want to show you, you will see it if we are real good theatre workers.

What does the device do? you ask.

How does it act?

It does this: it turns in part or whole to receive the play of light.

I would sum up the whole matter in these words.

– Then it is all a matter of the light?

Let us not be in too great a hurry with our 'all a matter of' – I am afraid I cannot say that it is *all* a matter of any *one* thing.

Simplicity and elaboration are not arrived at by any quicker process than that by which a perfect runner or a perfect swimmer achieves the simplification and elaboration necessary to outstrip the others . . . and with the runner and swimmer it is not all a matter of this or that . . . it is a matter of attending to a hundred things all the time.

Let us go on. In creating a scene for a drama which is worth hearing and worth seeing, we have never to forget what the spectators require.

One of the first of their demands is that they shall be able to see and hear the actor as he performs before us, especially his face (or mask) – and his hands and person.

Therefore any theory which attempts to state the uses of light in relation to scene without stating the use of light to the acting is value-less.

Here then are a few general facts which it is useful to remember.

1. You can see a face – a hand – a vase – a statue better when it is backed by a flat plain non-coloured surface than when backed by something on which a coloured pattern or some other object is painted or carved.

2. The shadow of a thing (face, hand, or statue) is visible to the eye without difficulty or distraction, and is visible at the same time as is the thing itself.

3. When the face, hand, or statue is removed, a plain screen is a dull thing to look at – the eye tires.

4. The eye cannot look at two objects at the same time. When we listen to a speaker, be it in a room or in a hall or in a theatre, we look at one thing only – his face.

5. In a theatre our eyes follow the speaker; therefore when two are speaking it is usual and it is best for these two to be as near one another as possible.

6. It is essential they shall be in sympathy in their work. Any division in this and we shall at once feel the division and see neither of the actors – our thoughts will wander to the scenery.

7. The screen against which an actor is best seen is a white one – for it can be shaded to any tone of grey, blackened by shade; coloured any colour, and that without changing the colour of the actor's face, hands, or figure.

8. There is no need at all for any actor's face to be cast into shadow and the expression lost until it loses distinction of expression . . . then, indeed, it seems best to blot it out.

9. There was never any need of scenery to take an overdue prominence until the day when the actor lost his power of expression, his power to act, and until he began to resent the right uses of scene and light.

10. The use of light to the actor is that it will aid him and collaborate with him if he will show it consideration. For light can be used in many dramatic ways – it is for the actor to come to know at least fifty or eighty of these ways. At present he acknowledges about six.

11. The use of light to the actor is only to be studied by the actor if he

will observe the way light plays its subtle part in real life. If he will
observe he will soon come to realise that stage lighting can be his best
friend in his work. As an aid to his observation the treatise by Leonardo da Vinci on light can help an actor sufficiently advanced in his
studies.

Having stated some of the uses of light to the actor, I can now
proceed to state the relation of light to this scene.

The scene turns to receive the play of light.

These two, scene and light, are, as I have said, like two dancers or
two singers who are in perfect accord.

The scene supplies the simplest form made up of right angles and
flat walls and the light runs in and out and all over them.

The scene is not merely put up (though it stands on its own feet by
the way) on the stage without thought of *how* it be placed and some
light turned on without considering *what* light – whence it comes – and
what it sets out to do.

In the *placing* of the scene, and in the *turning* to receive the light,
and in the *placing* and *directing* of the light lie the little difficulties.

Again, the relation of light to this scene is akin to that of the bow to
the violin, or of the pen to the paper.

For the light *travels* over the scene – it does not ever stay in one
fixed place, ... travelling it produces the music. During the whole
course of the drama the light either caresses or cuts, – it floods or it
trickles down, – it is never quite still though often enough its movement
is not to be detected until an Act has come to an end, when, should we
have any power of observation left (and drama should cure us of any
furtive desire to observe), we find our light has changed entirely.

Scene and light then move.

I may have any number of pieces in my scene and I may have any
number of lamps. . . .

The text is read at the pace at which it will be delivered, and at each
appointed cue a single or a double leaf of my screen moves – at the
same time one of my lamps will begin to play its light at a given strength
and from a given position and in a given direction.

At each cue another leaf or other leaves turn – advance – recede –
fold up or unfold – imperceptibly, or maybe on some occasions
markedly, while at the same time other lamps will begin to function,
move their position, change their strengths, alter their direction.

My screens can pass from and to any spot on the stage floor and
nothing obstructs their passage.

My light can pass from and to any position in the air or on the stage and so play upon any spot I require.

How these two simple deeds are performed I will show you, with diagrams making it quite clear, the year after I have shown you their performance in several plays.

I regret very much that I cannot show them to you here and now . . . but were I to do so my lighting and its simple device would be quickly caught up by some ever-ready theatre manager or one of his assistants, who would put the thing before you in a manner which I think might satisfy the groundlings to whom Shakespeare alludes, but which I am sure would not satisfy you.

So this is one of those devices which I shall keep for you until we are allowed a theatre – you to come into as spectator, I to work in 'at your service' as artist.

It is enough to add that I can light the face, hands, and person of any given actor, be he in any part of the stage, and without lighting the scene, and I can paint with light any part of the scene without obliterating the actor for a moment.

And I could not say that eight years ago.

I am enabled to say so now because I have discovered how to do this in the course of the last four years.

The further question, whether it is desirable and necessary *always* to light the actor at every moment of the play with the same quantity of light is one which I today believe may have to be gone into *with* the actor . . . no one is more reasonable than he when the theatre is open and running smoothly.

A little more is to be said and I am done.

I can colour my screens or the actor's form to a great extent in the same degree and with the same strength and quality as a painter uses on his canvas. I employ only light . . . he employs his paints.

I am limited by my medium as he is by his, and both of us have to obey our particular tools and materials. – He cannot do anything beyond paint on a flat surface in colours – I can do no more than project my light on to my screens and figures.

But whereas he had his materials and tools discovered for him and a method of long-standing taught him, I have had to find out my materials and tools, and I have been obliged to invent a method for using them.

Therefore, if I have not yet reached as perfect a method of using these things as he has, and if I cannot reach it before I am obliged to give up the work, others to whom I shall leave my plans and experiments must continue on after I have done and discover better ways if they can.

It is for this serious reason, so as to preserve, so as not to lose what discoveries I have made, that I very much hope I shall have a workshop and enough assistants who can carry on this work after my death. To no others will I entrust what I hope I am not too presumptuous in considering of value.

This page remains as a testimony that I announced my need of these things and that I was given the means to preserve my discoveries for those who come after me.

Or it may serve as a testimony to the contrary.

from *The Thousand Scenes in One Scene* (*1915*)

THE 'SCENE' AND THE POETIC DRAMA
The highest form of modern theatrical art is the performance of the poetic drama. It neither reaches the altitudes of the old religious drama nor falls to the splendid depths of the musical comedy, but is something betwixt and between, and it is considerably nearer to the higher than the lower.

Thus everyone must acknowledge that there is much of the modern musical comedy and melodrama in Shakespeare, but that there is more spiritual drama. Shakespeare even condescends to the touch of the music hall and is at home in it, but from it he is continually rising to touch those heights called by some . . . the impossible.

It is for this poetical drama that the scene which is the subject of this article was created.

Since making it its creator has felt that it will be of service not only to the theatre, but also to the dramatic poet; and hopes that both to the stage and to the poet it will prove of great practical use, . . . using the word 'practical' in its fullest signification.

Its practical use has been already not only demonstrated before poets, but proved in a theatre before an audience, and in the third section of my article I shall set forth this practical value in detail; that is to say, I shall show how it saves time, space, force and money.

Of its other practical aspect I will treat in the next section and will there show the practical or technical artistic advantages which it possesses over modern scenery.

A Warning First of all it is necessary to state that this scene is an invention patented by its inventor, and that the imitation of some of its

EXTERNAL and SUPERFICIAL QUALITIES by the trade, and recorded by pictures in *The New Movement in the Theatre*, Mr Sheldon Cheney's useful book, are to be mistrusted. Only genuine works of art have any ultimate value commercially or artistically: imitations and spurious copies are for the gull.

Description of the Scene   The scene is made up usually of four, six, eight, ten or twelve screens, and, although sometimes of more than twelve, seldom of less than four. Each part or leaf of a screen is alike in every particular except breadth, and these parts together form a screen, composed of two, four, six, eight or ten leaves. These leaves fold either way and are monochrome in tint.

The height of all these screens is alike.

These screens are self-supporting and are made either of a wooden frame covered with canvas, or of solid wood.

With screens of narrow dimensions curved forms are produced, for larger rectangular spaces broader leaved screens are used, and for varied and broken forms all sizes are employed.

Sometimes a flat roof is used with these screens, at other times the space above the top line is shown.

The scene being monochrome, the minimum of light is required to illuminate it, as there is much reflection from each leaf. Ordinary battens that are used in the theatre, and also daylight, can be used for its illumination.

The screens can be so arranged that by moving three leaves a great change in effect is produced.

The art of using this scene to the best advantage is a delicate one and acquired only with practice. The aim of the arranger is to place his screens in such a position that, by moving the minimum number of leaves, he may produce the desired amount of variety. Where the maximum amount of variety is required the change is less easy to accomplish, for, in art as well as in nature, sudden contrasts cause more trouble because, as a rule, undesirable.

Sometimes certain additions may be made to this scene, such as a flight of steps, a window, a bridge, a balcony, and of course the necessary furniture, though great care and reserve must be exercised in making these additions so as to avoid the ridiculous.

Artistic Values   This scene is a living thing.

In the hands of an artist it is capable of all varieties of expression, even as a living voice and a living face are capable of every expression.

The scene remains always the same, while incessantly changing.

Some may ask how such a thing can possibly be, and one can only ask such questioners to study the human face.

Every human face is shaped more or less the same, and is made up of two eyes, a brow, a nose, a mouth, a chin and so forth; move any one of these parts ever so little, and we note a different expression.

This scene resembles the human face.

It is obvious that the advantage of such a scene will be best understood and felt by those who see it; but its uses can at any rate be recorded to some advantage.

Through its use we obtain a sense of harmony and a sense of variety at the same time. We may be said to have recovered one of the unities of the Greek drama without losing any of the variety of the Shakespearean drama.

We pass from one scene to another without a break of any kind, and when the change has come we are not conscious of any disharmony between it and that which is past.

I have said of this scene that it is a living thing, that it is capable of expression and I must here warn you, from personal experience in its use, that it is so living that, unless treated as a living thing, it is quite likely not to respond to the will of the manipulator or arranger.

Accidental effects can be obtained which are beautiful even as a beautiful accidental effect can be produced on a piano, but no one without knowing this scene intimately, that is to say, without having studied it more than carefully, can produce harmony from its planes. It even refuses to obey the artist entirely when the artist is not in the right mood; and its inventor has worked with a set of screens for a day or two searching for an especial form for a screen in *Hamlet* and been totally unable to bring out any expression from its flatness; yet in the process of overcoming the difficulty perhaps a more perfect harmony has been ultimately produced.

The results obtained have found favour with all the poets, a few of the actors, all the stage managers and some of the directors of theatres to whom they have been shown, and the scene has also won the approval of the stage hands, whose praise the inventor values. To all of these he declares himself beholden for many suggestions which have improved the instrument.

Advantages to Actor and Stage Manager   Now one of the advantages of this invention is that, should the actor feel after a few nights that he could play the scenes better in a different arrangement, and have a clear idea as to his wishes and how to obtain them, he can test his ideas in the morning on the model and make his changes that same evening.

If after a month or so he wishes to change again, either because he thinks something can be improved by giving himself more liberty as actor, or for any other reason, he can again make any change which seems to him desirable. In fact the scene is as much for the actor as it is for the stage manager or the poet.

If the actor feels that he cannot play his part in a certain scene he has only to go to the stage manager, and together, with the model on the table, they can work out a new arrangement.

The advantages which the use of this model offers to the stage manager are exceptional.

The Model Stage and Scene To begin with, the model with which he works is always ready to his hand. He keeps it in his study and is thus able continually to test ideas which come into his head as to the poetic drama which he has to produce. He has not to wait for the scene painter to bring him a model which, if he does not like, he has to have changed and rechanged; but he has at his disposal a model scene which he can be always changing and arranging, and from which he can derive ideas for the movement of his figures.

Possessing the model, he is not saddled with a cumbersome and elaborate 'model stage' of the usual pattern; he need not fear to touch the thing lest it fall to pieces, or the strings and wires get tangled. He has a workman-like model to use . . . no litter, no strings, no paper; no longer a toy but clean and solid wood.

He is often at a loss how to fashion scenes for these old plays which have held the boards for so long. In his study he fancies a passage here, a long wall somewhere there, pillars here; but he is unable to put these down on paper, and if he could do so it would still be unsatisfactory. He could not see the thing, he could not measure his distances, he could not tell whether there is enough space for a man to come on there, whether there will be room enough on the stage for this passage to go back in that direction, and in his helplessness he is obliged to tell the scene painter to make the design. But with the scene which is here offered him, and with this small model stage all this preliminary work will be made many times easier. He can do it himself.

He is producing *Richard III* for instance. He wants a vast throne-room for the one scene and he wants to follow it up by a small cell. He can place his screens upon his model stage, and turn them this way and that until he has got his throne room. He can then mark the results down upon the ground-plan drawn to scale with which the inventor provides him.

After he has done this he can move one or two leaves of the screen so as to bring all the screens to form a smaller, prison-like place.

At the first attempt he will not have much success. He will then probably begin by forming the smaller scene first and he will try if it is not possible to work backwards, passing from the second to the first scene, from the smaller to the larger instead of from the larger to the smaller. He may probably find that this makes his task easier.

But he who finds the greatest difficulty at the outset in arranging scenes from these screens is more likely than another to produce ultimately more important results if he persevere; but one should avoid if possible the feeling that there is something very difficult about the manipulation of the scene.

Some say that this is the poet's scene. To a certain extent in its first state it is more his scene than anyone else's, for it represents the world perhaps better than any other scene has done ... that particular world created by the poets, the world of imagination. The poets themselves have said so.

But let not the casual reader think that this indicates something flimsy and floating. Nothing of the kind. It is something sharp-cut, something vivid and definite, as firm in its outline as it is flexible in its movement, and this, I believe, is what the poets have always held such a world to be.

Finally, in connection with this scene the inventor has planned several additional inventions by means of which doors, windows, cornices, staircases, trees, hills, clouds, stars, sun, moon and all can be placed before the audience, and that without calling in a single extra man to assist the usual staff.

Practical Values of this 'Scene'   To save unnecessary waste of money and time is the aim in the organisation of every enterprise. It is more often than not that this idea of true economy is forgotten in the theatre, and is substituted by waste.

Mr Fitzroy Gardner, a keen theatrical manager, writing in the *Strand Magazine* says, 'I have no hesitation in saying that in the West End theatres of London at least forty thousand pounds a year are frittered away, apart from what is lost by putting on plays with a four-to-one chance against their success. . . . Scenery and dresses are often ordered without proper deliberation, or negotiations as to cost.'

Much power of all kinds is wasted in the theatre, and in no department is there greater waste than in the scenic department.

The scenery has always wasted the time of the theatre, of the actors, of everyone, more especially in productions of the popular drama. Scenery has also wasted the receipts of the theatre. Scenery has always wasted the energies and force of the managerial staff; it has also wasted space. Large warehouses are costly and the space on the stage is valuable.

So we see clearly that time, force, space and money are wasted by modern scenery, whereas all four are economised by the use of this scene.

Under these four headings of time, force, space and therefore money, let us enumerate some of its advantages, and show in what way economy is possible through its use.

The Saving of Time   Time. It saves the manager's time, for after he has once mastered its simple mechanism he is able in a short time to produce arrangements with his model which shall give the effect he requires. It also saves him the time which would otherwise be spent in discussing plans and models with the scene painters, carpenters and workmen.

The fact that the scene is self-supporting saves the time which is usually wasted in hanging scenery and in finding spare places for the accommodation of the different cloths, cut-cloths, built-out pieces, etc.

It saves the manipulator's time as, the screens being easy to move from one position to another, one full set can change to another full set in less than thirty seconds.

The maximum wait between the acts need not exceed seven minutes at most, and it can even be less if desired. Eighteen men can strike the largest set and leave the stage empty in twenty seconds. A smaller change can be effected in four to ten seconds by fewer men. It is greatly owing to the fact of each screen being self-supporting that this becomes possible. It also saves time in all that concerns the lighting.

Time is wasted in rehearsing the lights because such rehearsal in so many instances means guessing which light is best; here it is saved because the simplest light is the best; that is to say, the light of the battens. The inventor tells us that, whereas in former experiments he usually did away with the battens, he has found they work perfectly easily with this scene. It has been continually demonstrated, in fact, that no other light is so good.

Another saving of time in regard to the lighting is that the manager can calculate with more precision than formerly the necessary strength of his limes.

We come then to the advantages in the matter of storage.

It is a great saving of time here also to be able to store this scene in the theatre itself, for as a rule much time is wasted in sending to the warehouse for the heavy scenery of the popular drama, and on the continent even more time is lost in this labour than in England owing to the nightly changes. But in any theatre where the programme is changed a great saving of time is effected through the use of this scene.

The Saving of Force and Labour Labour. Under this heading are included both mental and physical labour. The manager is saved the mental strain of interviewing and discussing plans with many different persons because he has only to give them the finished plan to carry out when he has worked it out upon his model, and this working out he can do with greater quiet and concentration in his own study by himself than when obliged to do it in the usual way with the scene painters, carpenters and others upon the stage.

In fact, force and labour are saved to the manager and the staff right through the production of the play, because they know that their model is a thing with which they can calculate.

If this scene were like ordinary scenery, . . . that is to say, not self-supporting, every time it moved its position it would have to be attached to ropes or supports of some kind which would necessitate the expenditure of energy not required when the thing is self-supporting. The force necessary to manipulate the modern scenery for a big production is enormous, whereas to move these six or ten screens and their additional parts which compose the scene is a very easy matter and a great saving in physical force.

It is probably for this reason that it has found such favour with the workmen who have already used it.

The Saving of Space Space. Space is economised because the scene takes up no room in the flies, since, instead of being slung, it is self-supporting and when finished is folded up and goes easily into the scene dock, taking up the minimum of storage room.

There is the same economy of space in the transport of scenery from town to town for which, with ordinary scenery, many railway trucks are needed; but much space is saved in the transport of this scene owing to the fact that the measurements of all its parts are standardised.

There are 805 theatres in England, not counting the music halls, nor the small platforms or drill halls which are used for play acting and for concerts. The small places cannot afford to buy much scenery; this is often the reason why plays are not produced in the small places.

This screen scene is elastic. When placed on the stage it can be compressed or enlarged. A small theatre purchases, say, four small screens for its first productions. Next year it can add to that number two more, and two more the following year. So at the end of three years it has eight screens. Each addition to it makes a new combination possible while the original effects obtained and the original arrangements devised remain as useful as ever they were.

The Saving of Money   Money. It saves money because time, labour and space are saved by its use and the waste of all these things costs money.

This scene, as I have already said, goes into one or two trucks. This indicates how much room it takes and therefore not more than the same amount of room is needed if it is ever to be stored outside the theatre.

Owing to its being monochrome the minimum amount of light is sufficient, the leaves of the screens acting as reflectors.

Lastly the adaptability of these few screens to many plays so that an infinite variety of effects can be obtained . . . and those effects more artistic in quality than usual . . . makes it obvious to everyone that the saving in the expenditure on scenery is considerable.

To be able to put the scenery for *Hamlet, Faust, The Merchant of Venice, The Taming of the Shrew, The Tempest, The Bourgeois Gentilhomme, Rosmersholm*, and *When We Dead Awaken, Pelleas and Melisande, Phédre, Elektra*, The *Agamemnon, Salome, Œdipus Rex, The Land of Heart's Desire, La Gioconda* . . . to be able to put all the scenery for these plays in one or two railway trucks proves that the cost must be very much less than that of the ordinary scenery which would require ten or fifteen trucks at the very least.

There is also the initial saving in expenditure in the purchase of scenery, since instead of a complete set for each play one set may be used for all. In fact this scene may from all points of view be described as '*Multum in parvo*'.

On the ground of its practicality patents have been obtained in Europe, including Germany, and in America, and, after having experimented with the full sized models which have been made in Moscow and in London, it has been found that it answers all expectations and fulfils every requirement of the popular drama.

In fact it has proved economical both artistically and commercially, and the European managers before whom it has been tested confirm this estimate of its value.

It will be of interest here to quote the two following extracts from *The Times* (London), the former written after a 'demonstration' of the use of the scene by its inventor, at his studio in London in 1911; the latter an extract from the account sent by *The Times*' special correspondent in Moscow, after the first production of *Hamlet* with the screen scenery, at the Arts Theatre in that city. The *Hamlet* production has since then been already given over one hundred and fifty times in the same theatre.

September, 23, 1911.

The device is extremely simply. It consists of folding screens, which will stand of themselves without being fastened either to the stage or to ropes, rollers, or beams in the 'flies'. The screens can be made of any size required. They may be 30ft. high or only 8ft.; they may have three folds or a dozen, and each fold may be 1ft. wide or 6ft. Three men in three minutes could move or remove a whole scene and, folded flat, each screen would take up very little space. The obvious advantages are the ease and quickness with which these things can be handled and the simplicity of the manipulation. To change a scene would no longer be to roll up or roll down great canvases, to screw and unscrew bolts, to adjust and fasten ropes, to remove entirely an elaborate built-up set, and put another in its place. A complete change of scene can be obtained merely by rearranging a few screens. And when it is necessary (as in the case of touring companies) to take away the complete scenery of a play, the carpenters, instead of working all night and losing some very important piece of the outfit, could transport the folded screens to the van at a reasonable hour. Moreover, that terror of Monday morning in provincial theatres . . . the 'scene-plot' . . . is reduced to a simple plan of the stage marked out in squares with the positions of the screens shown by letters or figures, and a quarter of an hour's work ought to make the whole set of changes clear to the stage-hands.

Ease and quickness of manipulation are matters that interest the public no less than the stage-manager and scene-shifters. On the playing of Shakespeare, for instance, such a device would have wide and deep effects. But the question most likely to occur to the public first of all is what kind of scenery these screens provide. Not, of course, the scenery of detail and archaeology, the scenery of crowded fact and 'realisation of a period'. But an hour's experimenting with Mr Craig's model stage revealed a very wide variety of suggestions, moods, settings, properly so called, for drama. The model screens exhibited were all in monochrome, which was practically the 'self-colour' of the material of which the models were made; but indoor and outdoor scenes alike were made each in a few seconds and in two or three movements, and the purport of each was unmistakable. Quite extraordinary effects of space and spirit were obtained; and in this the lighting played a very important part. For one advantage of these screens is that the light can be directed

10. Bas relief
figure.
Iphigenia.
1907.

11. Bas relief figure.
Portia. 1909–1910.

12. Bas relief figure.
Four mourning figures for Greek Drama.
1907–1908.

13. From *Scene*. 1907.

14. From *Scene*. 1907.

15. From *Scene*. 1907.

16. From *Scene*. 1907.

17. *Hamlet* model with screens. 1912.

18. *The Pretenders.*
Eight small screens and a pallet bed. 1926.

19. *The Pretenders.* 1926.

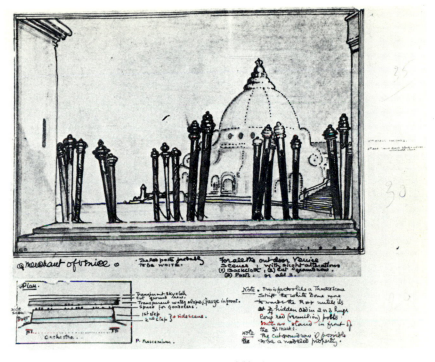

20. *The Merchant of Venice.* 1902.

21. *The Taming of the Shrew.* 1908.

22. *Macbeth*. 1906.

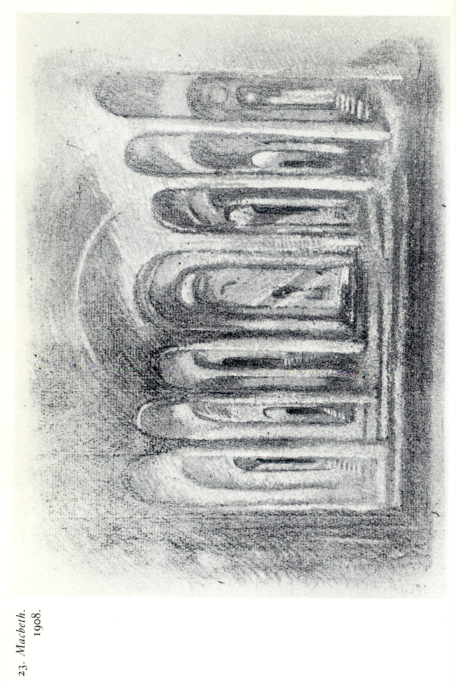

24. *Hamlet.* 1907.

from almost any point, and a change of light makes a change of mood, or even of place. Mr Craig's own desire appears to be to dispense as far as possible with any colouring on the screens themselves, partly because each screen can thus take on a much wider range of characters, so to speak, than if it were coloured. Most of the colouring would be obtained by means of coloured lights; and there would be no danger that a scene painted for one light would be robbed of its effect by being seen later under another light . . . an error too often made with scenery as we know it. Further definition . . . in a forest scene, for instance . . . can be obtained by means of an ingenious device for casting shadows; and 'properties' . . . chairs, tables, and the like . . . can be as easily used with these screens as with the curtains of the Elizabethans or with the built-up sets of the modern stage . . .

A street scene that would have done equally well for London, Florence, or Baghdad was made with three screens in three seconds; and there seems to be no reason why, with a sparing use of colour and pattern, a modern drawing-room should not be as clearly suggested as a castle or a magic island. A proscenium that can be easily enlarged or reduced forms a subsidiary part of the scheme; and sloping stages could, if necessary, be made flat for the reception of the screens.

It is claimed that the new scenery is cheap, easily and quickly provided, simply and quickly worked, and adaptable to practically all needs. It is certainly of wonderful effect in the suggestion of place and mood; and experiment with the models only whets the appetite to see a stage equipped with the new scenery on the full scale.

Moscow, January 9, 1912.

Every scene in the *Hamlet* has for its foundation an arrangement of screens which rise to the full height of the proscenium, and consist of plain panels devoid of any decoration. Only two colours are used . . . a neutral cream shade and gold. A complete change of scene is created simply by the rearrangement of these screens, whose values lie, of course, not so much in themselves as in their formation and the lighting.

Mr Craig has the singular power of carrying the spiritual significance of words and dramatic situations beyond the actor to the scene in which he moves. By the simplest of means he is able, in some mysterious way, to evoke almost any sensations of time or space, the scenes even in themselves suggesting variations of human emotion.

Take, for example, the Queen's chamber in the Castle of Elsinore. Like all the other scenes, it is simply an arrangement of the screens already mentioned. There is nothing which definitely represents a castle, still less the locality or period; and yet no one would hesitate as to its significance . . . and why? Because it is the spiritual symbol of such a room. A symbol, moreover, whose form is wholly dependent upon the action which it surrounds; every line, every space of light and shadow going directly to heighten and amplify the significance of that action, and becoming thereby something more than its mere setting . . . a vital and component part no longer separable from the whole. Whatever Mr Craig has done he has obviously done it not only with the touch of an artist, but also with all the care and reverence of a true lover of Shakespeare.

To judge from his work he is not so much a revolutionary as a reformer. Far from being an enemy to theatrical tradition, he seems to realise better than any one how much valuable material for his art lies buried in that limbo of things forgotten. He has gone back over a field whose fertility so many have ignored, and drawn from it all that is best and most useful to him.

5. Shakespeare

In the Foreword to *The Theatre Advancing* Craig mused on 'How to bring our English theatre to a condition which shall finally place it second to none in Europe.' His solution to the problem was 'to use every man and every talent and every penny to back our best horse'. The 'best horse' was, of course, Shakespeare.

In Shakespeare he found the perfect dramatist to suit his particular purpose, combining a theatre that was created by a member of a working company with an imagination which soared beyond the confines of everyday life. Craig acknowledged and even revelled in declaring that the plays were both perfect stage vehicles and unstageable. To those who have absorbed his words and pictures this paradox is not particularly difficult. That the plays of Shakespeare can offer a different aspect to each generation is one factor which has ensured their survival: this combined with their hardiness in the face of the butchery which the whim of certain periods has inflicted upon them.

Craig's designs for a number of Shakespeare's plays match writings which propose an atmospheric basis to interpretation and special emphasis. Drawings for *Hamlet* or at least for an aspect of *Hamlet* date back to when he was playing the part as an actor. He seems indeed to have given up acting with relief when he found that he could draw his response to a character with less effort than having to play him. If that is a fault it is a fault only in an actor, not in a director.

The drawings are often 'visions', freezing the action to encapsulate the essence of the scene. The production of *Hamlet* which he co-directed in Moscow, is well documented. He never directed *Macbeth* despite offering designs to Beerbohm Tree and for an American production which received decidedly cavalier treatment. The idea of *Macbeth* dominated by the supernatural is not only given life by possible settings but is spelled out in one of the most interesting of all his essays *On the Ghosts in the Tragedies of Shakespeare*.

For the rest the ideas speak for themselves, being sufficient to exasperate and alarm the Shakespeare industry as much as they ever did. We must be as thankful for that as we are regretful that, setting aside whose fault it was, he was able to stage no more of the Shakespeare corpus than he did. Had he directed more, perhaps he would have written less, and in an ephemeral art it is the documents which endure.

Shakespeare's Collaborators (1913)

How is it that the manuscript of Shakespeare's plays – over thirty plays – has never been found? How is it that not a page of his manuscript has been found? How is it that the manuscript has never reached us of a single page out of the thirty odd plays? It would have been a fine sight to see – this manuscript of which Ben Jonson tells us that not a line was blotted.

So curious a document should have been preserved. Who destroyed it? Who took care that not a single page of manuscript should be handed down for us to see?

Was it destroyed by Shakespeare? And if so, why was he so careful to destroy the manuscript when the plays were already printed?

I believe that it was destroyed by Shakespeare, and for a very natural reason which we shall come to later on, and because he was a very human being and more of a literary man than an actor.

Many people have felt that there is a mystery behind the authorship of the Shakespearean dramas, and if some few find satisfaction in shifting the authorship from one individual, the many are not so satisfied; and, if anything continue to seem mysterious, it is the simple fact that the whole series of dramas is something too colossal for one man to have created. Yet they cannot well see how two or three authors could sit year after year together and affably compose these turbulent, rollicking wonders.

I hazard a guess which is as much a guess as all the 'evidence' brought together in large volumes about Shakespeare. I believe that there is a mystery about the authorship of the plays, but not a very deep one; and that for this reason it has eluded those sappers – who have passed it while delving. I consider the mystery to be a subtle one, but not half so subtle as the Donellys and others would have us suppose.

In my opinion the dramas were created by Shakespeare in close collaboration with the manager of the theatre and with the actors; in fact, with practically the whole of the company who invented, produced, and acted them; and I believe that a glimpse of the manuscript of the plays would reveal a mass of corrections, additions, and cuts made in several handwritings. I believe that the improvisators – and the comedians of that day were great improvisators – contributed a great deal to the comedies, and not a little to several of the tragedies. I believe that the plays *grew* to their present literary perfection, three distinct periods marking their development.

The first period saw them sketched out; the second saw them acted – and at this period many speeches and even scenes were added from week to week, at rehearsal and after performances – and the third period saw them handed over to the poet for revision before being printed.

When first printed in a collection the plays were in a very different state from that in which they were spoken from the stage. I do not believe the same words were spoken at the performances in the theatre as were read by those who received them in even their earliest printed form.

Any one who has compared the two texts of *Hamlet* – that of 1603 and that of 1604 – cannot help being struck by one fact; that is, that the 1603 version reads like a stage play, and the 1604 version like a literary play. It has been polished for the reader.

Every alteration is the improvment of a literary stylist bent on being as faultless as possible; the literary Shakespeare is uppermost for the time, and he polishes with a vengeance, and even succeeds in polishing away some of the life. It is as though a Giovanni Bellini had been at work polishing a Van Gogh.

There seems no doubt to me that the polisher was Shakespeare, the non-theatrical Shakespeare. He seems determined to save his work – bent on clearing away the rubbish. He succeeds only too well, and clears away too much – and the stage pays for it.

Mark the short space of time between the rough and the polished versions! In the case of *Hamlet* it took him only a year to polish the drama, the year 1603.

If we believe that Shakespeare was the polisher, can we be equally sure that he was the sole creator of these tremendous works? I cannot.

I believe that he was employed at the theatre to write up any rough draft by professional or non-professional playwrights, and to work upon the shapeless dramas of older writers, or even that he filled in scenarios planned for the theatre by the directors.

But these were not the chief collaborators who worked with him upon the great series of thirty odd plays, the manuscript of which is utterly lost. His chief assistants were the actors.

That the poetry and beauty of some of the unique figures in the plays were born of Shakespeare's imagination I do not doubt, but I do most decidedly doubt whether the other part – the huge material side of the dramas – came from the poet. We should be less astounded at Shakespeare's accomplishment were his dramas less complete; if they lacked their grossness, their popular appeal, their naturalness, which, added to the sublimity of their poetic imagery, makes them seem too complete for one man to have created alone.

The naturalness of the dramas was, I believe, wafted to England from Italy. Italy had awakened just previous to the birth of Shakespeare to a new sense of drama. It was red-hot – spontaneous – natural. It appealed instantly, like the repartee of the peasants. There was something so natural about this new drama that its fitness was not decreased by the fact that hundreds of actors could give it birth. It was not a literary effort, quite the reverse. It was good talk, wonderful patter. There was life in every sentence uttered – life in every idea which poured out in a torrent of words – and often the highest distinction of expression.

I claim that Shakespeare's works are the fruit of a poet's collaboration with the newly formed dramatic art.

Let us take for example the comedy of *Much Ado About Nothing*, and especially the scenes between Beatrice and Benedick.

These, in my opinion, are all improvised. The manager having planned out the story – which he pieced together from old tales, or having a poor play on the Hero and Claudio story in his desk – puts the material into the hands of Shakespeare, with this direction: that he is to 'go easy' with the characters of Benedick, Beatrice, Dogberry, and Verges, for these four roles are to be played by the four first comedians, and these men know something about acting!

Shakespeare then sets to work. Hero and her story he elaborates lovingly, but leaves spaces when he comes to the comic scenes, and merely writes: 'In this scene Benedick and Beatrice meet and speak together'; or, 'Here Dogberry and the Watch'.

Next the play passes into rehearsal – two or three rehearsals at most – during which the four principal comedians arrange together a little what they shall talk about.

Then comes the performance, when, stimulated by the close and eager presence of the spectators, they carry out their plans and improvise further – brilliantly – usurping more than the share allotted to them by the playwright of action and interest. The framework of the play expands to fit them; the focus is altered. You will see that this has happened again and again in the other plays.

Perhaps you are aghast at what I suggest, and ask me heatedly if I mean really and seriously that during this first performance the two actors who played Benedick and Beatrice were capable of inventing on the spur of the moment – by the way, what a spur the spontaneous moment is to the true born actor! – that brilliant passage, commencing:

BEATRICE: I wonder you will still be talking, Signor Benedick! Nobody marks you.
BENEDICK: What, my dear Lady Disdain! Are you yet living?

I have the greatest pride in replying on behalf of the actors of the sixteenth century. Yes, they were equal to inventing that passage and very many others, such as the Benedick and Beatrice scenes, Act II, Scene I; and Act IV, Scene I; besides the Dogberry scenes in Acts III, IV, and V. All these, I consider, must in great part be attributed to the actors.

Indeed, much of the Elizabethan comedy is the work of the actors, produced in that spontaneous manner; many of those brilliant flashes of genius which have helped to give Shakespeare the position he holds today were first struck out in the sharp encounter of wits on the boards of the stage. But although we may quite easily believe this – as every one who has studied the history of the *Commedia dell'arte* will believe it – we may also be sure that the repartee was not exactly the same at the first as at the fiftieth performance. In fact, we may be positive that it varied very much at every performance; but during those representations the best part of the actors' improvisations were recorded by some scribe – perhaps even by Shakespeare – and written into the manuscript.

Later on, Shakespeare, knowing that the plays were to be published, took the whole play and polished it; and if he removed some of its spontaneity and doubtless some of its grossness, he left in the richest, cleverest part of the decoration which those actors of genius had contributed to the structure.

I feel certain that, placed as he was as playmaker-in-chief to the theatre, he determined to be revenged on all those secondary characters which were never able to hold the audience, being played by inferior actors while the chief players were doing things 'on their own'; that he waited his time, gathered together the strings of suggestion, and cleaned, tightened and made them beautiful by threading on them pearl after pearl of his poetry, each one more precious than another. But the strings – I claim them for those masters of improvisation, the actors; for the actors I claim part authorship of the world's masterpieces.

Two scenes where Benedick overhears his friends talking about Beatrice, and she overhears her friends talking about Benedick, are partly the creative work of the actors, partly that of the poet. In the second of these two scenes the poet has gathered together the gist of the speeches of the actors, and has given it to us again in a far more lovely form than it could ever have possessed originally. But if you remove many of these lovely passages of Beatrice you do not alter the shape of the play; in fact, you improve it somewhat if you condense it into the true drama. Hero and her story is far more important when we are not attracted away from her by the thought that perhaps Beatrice is a more poetic, a purer and a lovelier woman than all the Heros in the world.

Turning to other plays, who if not the actors invented the roles of Pistol (the Italian Capitano in an English dress), Bardolph, Lancelot Gobbo and old Gobbo, Doctor Caius (the Italian Dottore in a French dress), Sir Hugh Evans, Simple, Slender, Justice Shallow, Grumio, Biondello, Sir Toby Belch, Sir Andrew Aguecheek, Trinculo – and how many more? Not one actor – no Shakespeare-actor – invented them, but *actors*, a group collaborating, acting in unison, attempting each one to outdo the other, as it were to act the other off the stage.

If today actors cannot improvise, if wit and repartee have fled from the theatre to the music hall, from Mounet-Sully and Novelli to Lauder and Petrolini, it was not so in the fifteenth century. It was a Petrolini who invented Dogberry and a Lauder who created Launce – and no one knows how gross Launce was in 1600, though we may guess. And if any one doubt how brilliant the lighter comedians could be, those who would have played Benedick, Touchstone, and Malvolio, Beatrice and Rosalind, let him compare these records with the comedies of Molière, which likewise originated in the traditions of the *Commedia dell'arte*, by that time quite familiar to everyone in England and France.

Molière and Shakespeare are the despair of all later playwrights.

Let them despair no longer. They can do what Molière and Shakespeare did again and again; all they need is to find actors who will do half the great task for them. And let not the actors be any longer puzzled because they cannot get these Shakespearean sentences out of their mouths without choking; the Elizabethan polish once removed, all goes easily once more – it becomes plain English.

There can be, of course, no question of 'treating' Shakespeare's works in such a manner. They are best left as they were. But see how the instinct of every actor and every actor-manager leads him to cut away all the very highly polished bits, and – alas! – to deliver the rest in as

unpolished a manner as possible. Instinct on the stage counts for
something, and in this way the actor-managers, like hounds on the
scent of the fox, indicate clearly which way Reynard has escaped.

This is the secret which defies us; we wonder at the order of this
great group of plays, and at the same time at their irregularity. It does
not seem to us possible that the brain of one man, be he Shakespeare,
Bacon, or another, can have achieved such an overwhelming contradiction. The world-masterpieces are generally the product of many minds
– each sums up an age and humanity. Allow Shakespeare his contemporary fellow-workers, the actors, and the riddle becomes clear.

from *Index to the Story of My Days* (1957)

Romeo and Juliet was always a nerve-wracker for the audience – and for
me. They didn't like the love-making – neither did I. They would
whoop and cat-call at anything, because it got on their nerves. And
when Romeo, after getting the poison from the apothecary, tells the sky
that he is going back and will lie with Juliet tonight – meaning, naturally,
that he will kill himself with her, they whooped as though we had
somehow slipped through the fine net of the censor of plays.

Once, I remember, on this tour, the spectators even had an attack of
nerves in *Hamlet* – on seeing Hamlet holding a skull in his hands as he
said, 'Alas, poor Yorick!' I don't think the publishers will allow me to
put into print exactly what somebody yelled out; but evidently audiences are shaken by these very solemn things and it somehow doesn't
agree with them. Why Miss Baylis should have decided to *make* it agree
with them ('They *shall* come to heel, they *shall* like – what they don't
like') I have never been able to understand.

I think the idea of putting the whole of Shakespeare before the dear
old public is quite dreadful. I am all for a new interpretation of Shakespeare, quite different from what I once thought. I am now for filling
it with jolly tunes – especially *Hamlet* and the other very serious plays –
and twiddly dances and all sorts of comic touches. Also daring devices
'to entrap the wisest'.

For instance, I recently thought what an interesting thing it would be
if the part of Hamlet could be performed by an actor with a black
patch over one eye. I had a very good practical reason for suggesting
this to an old friend of mine, who was a very good actor, but who is not
now much before the public, and does not deserve to be. I said to
myself – and to him – 'If you played Hamlet with a black patch over
one eye, it would suggest a form of mourning which is ineffective, just

as Hamlet himself is ineffective – and there would be such an outcry at
the end of Act I, from critics and public alike, that you would be the
talk of the town, and *Hamlet* with you in it would run for two hundred
nights. Where would our Larry Olivier be then – where would Johnny
Gielgud be?' But my friend was actually shocked – he did not take the
suggestion seriously enough, and he had not enough courage either.

For if you come to think of it, people are sick and tired of seeing the
same Hamlet sitting in the same chair, with no marked sign of difference from any Hamlet seen before. And unless, century after century,
you can invest these well-known figures with visible characteristics that
have never been seen before, you will never arrest the five thousand
spectators who have to be arrested in order to listen. If boredom sets in
– I don't care if it is only drop by drop – from the commencement of
any one of these great plays, they and you are practically doomed to
suffer instead of being stimulated and enjoying them. And what, after
all, is so strange about Hamlet with a black patch? The answer is,
'Nothing is stranger.' Quite.

Now what is the advantage of Hamlet with a patch? It is that you
give the actor something which, if he plays on it properly, can be made
to speak 'with most miraculous organ'. I remember Irving, at a rehearsal
of *The Lyons Mail*, saying to Sam Johnson, 'What are you going to do
with this long scene, my boy?' Sam Johnson was a well-known actor,
playing the part of Choppard and being cross-questioned by the Judge
(played by Tyars). Old Sam Johnson didn't know what to do. And here
we get to the patch – only it wasn't a patch, it was a hat. Now how can
a hat play any part in a performance, except to be cocked on one side or
the other? Irving saw there was some way of making that hat speak, so
he said: 'Give me a hat.' They passed him a hat, he took it and began to
answer to the cues of this part, Choppard, with Johnson looking on.
And insofar as Irving brushed the hat this way, brushed it that way,
held it in front of him this way or laid his hand on the top of it that
way – I can't remember all the variety of things that his hands, face
and hat played all together – just so far did the whole hidden thoughts
of Choppard come to light. But, you see, without the hat he couldn't
have done it.

And I tried to point out to my friend the actor, 'Without this patch
you can't show all the things you would like to show.' I didn't confine
him to expressing only melancholy, I felt he could surely suggest twenty,
thirty, forty things by the way he handled this patch, by the significance
he gave to the wearing of it – first on one eye, then on the other,
perhaps – showing to one person his capacity to see quite well with it,

to another seeing nothing at all; by his scratching it or by his smoothing it. In fact there is nothing that such a 'property', as we call it, cannot be made to express. I have seen an actor do that with an eyeglass at the end of a string. We don't wear eye-glasses now, and I forget what the play was. But his manner of handling this glass was like a commentary, all the way through.

I think my friend objected to the patch because it would spoil his beauty. But I think he was very wrong not to take the plunge. 'You mustn't do such things.' Of course not – but every great actor has done them since the year one – and my dear friend would have become the rage. . . .

Hamlet and I had been together long and long before that . . . ever since I can remember . . . Hamlet almost seemed to me to be myself – yet I was not born a prince – nor a melancholy lad. But I came ever nearer and nearer to Hamlet, until he seemed to me if not to be myself – to be the nearest thing to me. So I sometimes suppose I was only Horatio.

Yes, this dear, strange, so easily understood nature – this Hamlet – and his mother – when as a young man I acted him I remember how much I loved my mother – I mean Queen Gertrude – I loved to be with her on the stage – but why was she so cross? The scenes where we were together, more especially in that lovely scene when there came to us into the room my father – his so pale and glaring eyes fixed upon us both. Poor dear – she, my mother I mean – she could not see him – she saw the chairs and the table – the bed – but not him – Heard nothing, heard only my words not his. (I suppose Shakespeare hadn't made a mistake, wasn't at all ga-ga) – and when he had left the room and it came to saying goodnight to her how sad, how very sad I felt – wept – yes indeed I wept, but silently, saying that when she wanted a blessing I'd beg a blessing of her.

And so in my life too – so I felt. Hamlet was not only a play to me nor he a role to be played – I somehow or other lived Hamlet day by day. Since I was so much like Hamlet myself I *had* to – not only were my weaknesses his, but his situation was almost mine.

I too had lost a father – I too saw my mother married to another – I exaggerated these things then and supposed my stepfather might well have poisoned him in his orchard at Harpenden as he slept. And sleeping, vanished. For one day I perceived that he was not there any longer – I needed him – and he only came in darkest visions – I sat ashamed alone – ashamed of what? I was always haunted by this father who was, yet was no longer there – and the longer it lasted the more I grieved.

Whisperers were around me – that I could hear – hear their whisperings and have to guess at the words.

Shakespeare's Plays (1908)

In a little book, which I published in 1905, I ventured to agree with those who hold the opinion that Shakespeare's plays were written for the reader and not for the stage. It seems many hold this opinion. Yet it was a satisfaction to me to come later across the following and other sentences in Goethe's writings –

> Shakespeare belongs by rights to the history of poetry; in the history of the theatre he only appears casually.
>
> Shakespeare's whole method of proceeding is one which encounters a certain amount of impracticability upon the actual stage.
>
> The very contractedness of the stage forces him to circumscribe himself.

Goethe comes to this conclusion, not at the beginning of his life but at the end of it, after his experience in the theatre has shown him that literature and the stage are, and must be, independent one of the other. I still remain of the same opinion – that Shakespeare's plays are not for representation, more especially because I am myself now working on several Shakespearean representations, and therefore have occasion for passing in review the many different 'editions', as they are called, of Shakespeare, especially the stage editions, and I am struck by one fact, and it is this: that the people who hold that Shakespeare was a master of theatrical art cut away from these plays lines, passages – nay, whole scenes: these words, passages and scenes which, they say, were written for the stage.

To say a thing is perfect and then to mutilate it, is most peculiar. If a manager wishes to cut a play, saying it will be better understood by the public if he does so, it is permissible provided he does not at the same time say that Shakespeare was a perfect master of dramatic art. Drama is for the people if ever an art was for the people, and if Shakespeare has not made himself clear to the people of all time, the actor-manager is not going to improve matters by cutting out large portions of the text.

In *Hamlet* it is usual for that long passage commencing, 'Now all occasions do inform against me', to be removed by the manager, who says that it does not 'help the play'. Now this is a most extraordinary state of affairs, that managers should be permitted to say what does or does not 'help the plays' of Shakespeare, after Shakespeare has himself

decided. Other passages in the play are removed because the managers
hold that they are indelicate or they hold that the audience would consider them indelicate. Cut the passage between Ophelia and Hamlet in
Act III, scene ii, when he is lying at her feet, and you rob the character
of Hamlet of very much of its force. Ophelia, instead of being a woman
of intelligence, becomes an early Victorian *débutante*; and Hamlet, instead of being a man of his time and suggesting a period which was
more than a period of manners, becomes a kind of preaching curate.

Of course the censor would object to this and other passages in Shakespeare, and he would be perfectly right, for the plays were not written
for the stage; they were written to be read. If you wish to act them act
them in their entirety or do not act them at all. It is as ridiculous to say
that the omission of a small passage is not going to harm such a work as
to say that the omission of so small a portion of the body as the eye
does not injure the whole.

This liberty with great plays is no sign of civilisation; it is barbarous
in the extreme. Another argument advanced for acting in this way is
that the performance must not last longer than a certain time. Time has
nothing to do with a performance. If it is good we do not mind how
long it takes: if it is bad it must be cut short, and therefore to advocate
a short time is to imply a fear on the part of the manager that the play
is going to be badly represented. Can one have too much of a good
thing? Then, too, it is quite possible to perform a play of Shakespeare
in its entirety in an evening provided the appliance for shifting the
scenery is not so absurdly elaborate that it takes twenty minutes to
change each act, and provided that the actors do not pause too long
over each syllable, but exercise their brains to think a trifle faster. It is
this slow delivery of Shakespeare's lines which has made Shakespeare a
bore to so many people. Here in the plays of Shakespeare we have
passionate scenes of an amazing description, more passionate than in
the Italian plays, and yet we drawl them and crawl them and are surprised when a Grasso comes to England and shows us how we should
speak, act and reveal the suddenness and madness of passion. We seem
to forget this fact, that passion is a kind of madness. We bring it to a
logical attitude and we deliver it with the voice of the judge or the
mathematician. It seems to have something to do with the totting up of
accounts; thus with us it is a shopman, not Othello, who is throttling
Desdemona. The emotional actors in England ought not to be content
with themselves for not waking up and sweeping all these too deliberate
and stodgy actors off the stage and out of the theatres.

Would the plays of Shakespeare be then interpreted as they should be? No, not even then. Not if the finest and most passionate actors in the world were to come together and attempt to perform *Hamlet* could the right representation of Hamlet be given, for I fear to represent *Hamlet* rightly is an impossibility. (1908)

Note: Yet since this was written, and since this book was first published in 1911, I have myself attempted to produce Hamlet – *the* Hamlet *of Shakespeare – at Moscow. Knowing it was impossible, why did I attempt it? There are many reasons: I wanted to strengthen my belief –I wanted people to realise the truth. Also, I wanted to 'face the music' – and I wanted to exercise my faculties as stage director (for I had not produced a play for many years). Added to this, I wanted to do what my friends wanted me to do.*

Was I satisfied? Yes. I am more thoroughly convinced than ever that the plays of Shakespeare are unactable – that they are a bore when acted – but also that the crowd loves nothing so well as a good confusion of principles in a theatre as they do in architecture, as they do in music. If you ask me whether the Moscow Art Theatre did well, I reply, Very, very well – but that it abided faithfully to principles, the principles which govern our art, is not the case.

Had it been true to principles it would have closed its doors three years ago, when I told its directors that this was the only right course open to it. Still it remains the first theatre in Europe – it reigns in Hell. (1912, E.G.C.)

from *Index to the Story of My Days* (1957)

FOR 1900
F. R. Benson had a season at the Lyceum Theatre. It seemed to me rather ridiculous. I saw him as Caliban in *The Tempest* . . . Benson's idea of Caliban was to come on stage with a fish between his teeth.

On *The Tempest* (1924)

The dreary puns and interminable conspiracies of Alonzo and Gonzalo and Sebastian and Antonio and Adrian and Francisco and other shipwrecked noblemen – Lytton Strachey.

It is when a wise reader and a fine writer says such a thing as this that we sit musing awhile, wondering.

I am wondering now whether Mr Strachey is quite right. This scene of the puns and the conspiracies in Act II of *The Tempest*, is it so dull, this scene? I have just reread it and find it, for all its length, curiously lively. Better than Act I, which, till Ferdinand's entrance, has been only struggling to awake and then wakes suddenly at the cry 'cock-a-diddle-dow'.

But I am wondering this too: wondering if these puns and conspiracy scenes should really prove to be dull; whether there would be great harm done for an inventive yet reverential stage manager to exert some of his cunning and by means of scene, voice and movement, by all and every means do what little he can to help Shakespeare out where he seems to be dreary, and thus quicken things a little?

You wince – you will have it that I am *miching mallecho*, that I mean mischief, *i.e.*, you frown with the wearisome thought of some more red fire and yet another transformation scene.

Listen; the dreary puns are issuing like bubbles from the mouths of six drowned live men sunken to the bed of the sea and wearily talking in their deadly sleep, Alonzo, Antonio, and the others.

Slowly they move, these deadly men, heavily like divers in deep seas; the sun pours through the pale blue green water so that it seems more like gentle air than many tons of water, and but for the coral around the sunken blocks of marble on which they sprawl, we should wonder whether we be in the air or the earth.

Lazily these once perfect *gentilomini* stretch themselves and sprawl, burbling out their rubbish, for here things are not going at breakneck speed as in Elsinore or Glamis: nor as in Milano: wrecked gentlemen with nothing to do are recovering some of their senses . . . they see a little . . . hear and speak – that is about all.

Were it not that one of these six men is bored I might be bored too – but while Sebastian swings his foot, 'sblood, I cannot close an eye, nor yawn. Here is someone I must watch: he was born to be remembered, yet for what I cannot say; still, I cannot forget him. He never stirs to any purpose; he is born and drowned for us in a play. A man so greatly at his ease, a prince, one who refuses to stir even when he suspects that he has somehow come into the wrong play, into a magic island too! His smile is not unlike the one worn by Charles Stuart, our second Charles.

There lie these six, shifting and sprawling in a forum in ruins, on these fallen blocks of marble which once stood up a city, now buried beneath the waves; slowly their wits return to them; only to be dull, to loaf and to sleep, to loll, and, one of them, to actually conspire. A wonderful act of awakening.

This magical island is somewhat of a scenical place with its songs and sprites and dancings and its quaint childlike devices of the stage carpenter; and, remembering that it was Shakespeare who took the part of Prospero when it was performed at Whitehall in 1611 (for so I believe was the case), and he aware of what he would have to face if he performed another operatic delight of this kind, is it at all strange that when it was over he should slip away after that Epilogue – you recall it – and much shaking of hands with some sixty or seventy odd fish of all kinds, and, getting to Stratford safe and sound, should swear to return no more to the purlieus of the accursed Whitehall?

Yet if to some of us as we read the play the island do never seem the gaudy-coloured theatrical place I have spoken of, if it seem more than this, if one is able to read and see no glare of any red fire and no glitter of spangles, but still see a magic island, what then?

A magic island.

Who has actually seen one, I or you, or neither? – yet an old and troubled mariner once came to me to tell of an island placed beneath the sea – a sunken island: I listened and I could not laugh: he stuttered on confusedly: and on, saying how he had lived down there for seven years; came back, he said, wearied with the life, but how came back no one could learn: '– then I came back', he kept repeating, and that was all.

In such an isle full fathoms five indeed our fathers lie.

And he spoke too of bells – bells of coral under the sea; 'Hark, now I hear 'em', he would often say, and stop to listen – 'Ding . . . dong . . . bell'.

'And what, . . . what did happen to you down there?' – I came as far as that one day with the old mad-man – this odd mariner.

He looked at me and made that steady settling gesture with his whole body which promises the beginning of a long tale, and his eye opened wider and he paused and drew the air slowly and slowly through his nostrils, held it a second – two seconds, looked long at me, and then lowering his eyes went away apparently eased of all his trouble at the perfect remembrance.

But leaving me very ill at ease.

What was it he saw down there – what was it that happened?

Something very beautiful to see and to hear must have been what he heard and saw.

Dull fish with cold eyes and bubbles issuing from their mouths, conspiring one with another as though it were London or Milano, that were not enough to charm this old man at the mere remembrance of it. Dead men and the wreckage of ships are nothing neither:

Something else was happening, something he will never forget . . .

168 *Craig on Theatre*

What was it?

What happened under the sea in an island known to none but he, is what I should like to make visible in *The Tempest* upon a stage, were I content to work to no purpose, to fashion what I fear would for ever fail to please you, you must perforce listen to 'the dreary puns and interminable conspiracies of Alonzo and Gonzalo and Sebastian and Antonio and Adrian and Francisco and other shipwrecked noblemen'.

from *The Artists of the Theatre of the Future* (1907)

Come now, we take *Macbeth*. We know the play well. In what kind of place is that play laid? How does it look, first of all to our mind's eye, secondly to our eye?

I see two things. I see a lofty and steep rock, and I see the moist cloud which envelops the head of this rock. That is to say, a place for fierce and warlike men to inhabit, a place for phantoms to nest in. Ultimately this moisture will destroy the rock; ultimately these spirits will destroy the men. Now then, you are quick in your question as to what actually to create for the eye. I answer as swiftly – place there a rock! Let it mount up high. Swiftly I tell you, convey the idea of a mist which hugs the head of this rock. Now, have I departed at all for one eighth of an inch from the vision which I saw in the mind's eye?

But you ask me what form this rock shall take and what colour? What are the lines which are the lofty lines, and which are to be seen in any lofty cliff? Go to them, glance but a moment at them; now quickly set them down on your paper; *the lines and their direction*, never mind the cliff. Do not be afraid to let them go high; they cannot go high enough; and remember that on a sheet of paper which is but two inches square you can make a line which seems to tower miles in the air, and you can do the same on your stage, for it is all a matter of proportion and nothing to do with actuality.

You ask about the colours? What are the colours that Shakespeare has indicated for us? Do not first look at nature, but look in the play of the poet. Two; one for the rock, the man; one for the mist, the spirit. Now, quickly, take and accept this statement from me. Touch not a single other colour, but only these two colours through your whole progress of designing your scene and your costumes, yet forget not that each colour contains many variations.

On the Ghosts in the Tragedies of Shakespeare (1908)

A very curious indication as to the way in which the producer should treat the Shakespearean tragedies on the stage lies in the appearance in those tragedies of the ghosts or spirits.

The fact of their presence precludes a realistic treatment of the tragedies in which they appear. Shakespeare has made them the centre of his vast dreams, and the central point of a dream, as of a circular geometrical figure, controls and conditions every hair's breadth of the circumference.

These spirits set the key to which, as in music, every note of the composition must be harmonised; they are integral, not extraneous parts of the drama; they are the visualised symbols of the supernatural world which enfolds the natural, exerting in the action something of that influence which in 'the science of sound' is exerted by those 'partial tones, which are unheard, but which blend with the tones which are heard and make all the difference between the poorest instrument and the supreme note of a violin'; for, as with these, 'so in the science of life, in the crowded street or market place or theatre, or wherever life is, there are partial tones, there are unseen presences. Side by side with the human crowd is a crowd of unseen forms. Principalities and Powers and Possibilities. . . . These are unseen but not unfelt. They enter into the houses of the human beings that are seen, and for their coming some of them are swept and garnished, and they abide there, and the last state of these human beings is radiant with a divine light and resonant with an added love; or, on the contrary, it may be that, haunted by spirits more wicked than themselves, the last state of such beings is worse than before: subject to a violence and tyranny abhorrent even to themselves; impalpable and inevitable as it would seem, even to the confines of despair.' [Shorthouse]

It is by the necromancy of these 'partial tones', by the introduction of influences felt even when unseen, at times impalpable as the 'shadow of a shadow', yet realised even then as dominant forces, sometimes malefic, sometimes beneficent, that Shakespeare achieves results which surpass those of his contemporaries even when, like Middleton in his *Witch*, they treat of similar themes.

For when Shakespeare wrote, 'enter the ghost of Banquo', he did not have in his mind merely a player clothed in a piece of gauze. Nor had he done so, had he been preoccupied with gauze and limelight, would he ever have created the Ghost in *Hamlet*; for that ghost of Hamlet's father, who moves aside the veils at the beginning of the great play, is not a joke; he is not a theatrical gentleman in armour, is not a farce of a figure. He is a momentary visualisation of the unseen forces which dominate the action and is a clear command from Shakespeare that the men of the theatre shall rouse their imagination and let their reasonable logic slumber.

For the appearances of all these spirits in the plays are not the inventions of a pantomime manager; they are the loftiest achievements of a lofty poet, and carry to us the clearest statements we can ever receive as to Shakespeare's thoughts about the stage.

'The suggestive shall predominate, for all pictures on the stage pretending to illusionise reality must necessarily fail in their effect or cause a disillusionment. Shakespeare's dramas are poetic creations and must be presented and treated as such'; [Hevesi] advice which should be especially borne in mind by all who set themselves to interpret those of the plays in which the supernatural element is introduced.

Thus if a man of the theatre shall produce *Macbeth, Hamlet, Richard III, Julius Caesar, Antony and Cleopatra, The Tempest,* or *A Midsummer Night's Dream* as they should be produced, he must first of all woo the spirits in those plays; for unless he understand them with his whole being he shall but produce a thing of rags and tatters. The moment, however, that he is at one with these spirits, the moment he has seen their proportion and moved to their rhythm, in that moment is he a master of the art of producing a play by Shakespeare. But this the stage manager never seems to realise, for did he do so he would adopt a very different method for the interpretation of those scenes in which the ghosts appear.

For what is it makes the ghosts of Shakespeare, which are so significant and impressive when we read the plays, appear so weak and unconvincing on the stage? It is because in the latter case the tap is turned on suddenly, the right atmosphere has not been prepared.

Enter a ghost – sudden panic of all the actors, of all the limelights, of all the music and of the entire audience. Exit the ghost – intense relief of the whole theatre. In fact, with the exit of the ghost on the stage the audience may be said to feel that something best not spoken about has been passed over. And so the mighty question, which is at the roots of the whole world, of life and death, that fine theme ever productive of so much beauty and from which Shakespeare weaves his veils, is slurred over, avoided as with an apologetic cough.

We are children in such matters. We think a bogie will do. We giggle when we are asked to present the idea of something spiritual, for we know nothing of spirits, disbelieving in them. We giggle like children and wrap ourselves in a table-cloth and say 'wow, wow, wow'. Yet consider such plays as *Hamlet, Macbeth, Richard III.* What is it gives them their supreme mystery and terror, which raises them above mere tragedies of ambition, murder, madness and defeat? Is it not just that supernatural element which dominates the action from first to last; that blending of the material and the mystical; that sense of waiting figures intangible as death, of mysterious featureless faces of which, sideways, we seem to catch a glimpse, although, on turning fully round, we find nothing there? In *Macbeth* the air is thick with mystery, the whole action ruled by an invisible power; and it is just those words which are never heard, just those figures which seldom shape themselves more definitely than a cloud's shadow, that give the play its mysterious beauty, its splendour, its depth and immensity, and in which lies its primary tragic element.

Let the stage manager concentrate his attention and that of his audience on the seen things which are temporal, and such a play is robbed of half its majesty and all its significance. But let him introduce, without travesty, the supernatural element; raise the action from the merely material to the psychological, and render audible to the ears of the soul if not of the body 'the solemn uninterrupted whisperings of man and his destiny', point out 'the uncertain dolorous footsteps of the being, as he approaches, or wanders from, his truth, his beauty or his God', and show how, underlying *King Lear*, *Macbeth* and *Hamlet*, is 'the murmur of eternity on the horizon,' [Maeterlinck] and he will be fulfilling the poet's intention instead of turning his majestic spirits into sepulchral-voiced gentlemen with whitened faces and robes of gauze.

Consider, for instance, more in detail, the play of *Macbeth*, in which 'the overwhelming pressure of preternatural agency urges on the tide of human passion with redoubled force'. [Hazlitt] The whole success of its representation depends upon the power of the stage manager to suggest this preternatural agency and on the capacity of the actor to submit to the tide of the play, to that mysterious mesmerism which masters Macbeth and his 'troop of friends'.

I seem to see him in the first four acts of the play as a man who is hypnotised, seldom moving, but, when he does so, moving as a sleep-walker. Later on in the play the places are changed, and Lady Macbeth's sleep-walking is like the grim, ironical echo of Macbeth's whole life, a sharp, shrill echo quickly growing fainter, fainter, and gone.

In the last act Macbeth awakes. It almost seems to be a new role. Instead of a sleep-walker dragging his feet heavily he becomes an ordinary man startled from a dream to find the dream true. He is not the man some actors show him to be, the trapped, cowardly villain; nor yet is he to my mind the bold, courageous villain as other actors play him. He is as a doomed man who has been suddenly awakened on the

morning of his execution, and, in the sharpness and abruptness of that
awakening, understands nothing but the facts before him, and even of
these understands the external meaning only. He sees the army in front
of him; he will fight, and he prepares to do so, puzzling all the time
about the meaning of his dream. Occasionally he relapses into his state
of somnambulism. While his wife lived he was not conscious of his
state, he acted the part of her medium perfectly, and she in her turn
acted as medium to the spirits whose duty it ever is to test the strength
of men by playing with their force upon the weakness of women.

Nietzsche, writing of Macbeth, sees only the mad ambition of the
man, this human passion of ambition; and he tells us that this sight,
instead of irresistibly detracting from the evil ambition in us, rather
augments it. Perhaps this is so; but it seems to me that behind all this
there is much more than evil ambition and the idea of the hero and the
villain.

Behind it all I seem to perceive the unseen forces already spoken of;
those spirits that Shakespeare was always so fond of hinting stood
behind all things of this earth, moved them, and moved them apparently
to those great deeds for good or evil.

In *Macbeth* they are called by the old grandmother's title of the
Three Witches, that elastic name which the public in the theatre may
either laugh at or be serious about as it wishes.

Now when I speak of this hypnotic influence of these spirits as
though I were mentioning something quite new, I am speaking entirely
in relation to the interpretation of Shakespeare on the stage and not
merely as his student. I know that the students have written about these
spirits, comparing them to certain figures in the Greek tragedy and
writing of them far more profoundly than I can do. But their writings
are for those who read Shakespeare, or who see him acted, not for
those who take part in the presentation of his plays. Whether the plays
were ever intended to be acted or no, whether or not they gain by being
acted, does not concern me here. But if I were asked to present this
play of *Macbeth* upon the stage, I should need to bring to it an understanding different entirely from that which the student brings when he
has only himself to consider as he sits reading it in private. You may
feel the presence of these witches as you read the play, but which of
you has ever felt their presence when you saw the play acted? And
therein lies the failure of the producer and the actor.

In *Macbeth* it is, to my mind, during the hypnotic moments that we
should feel the overpowering force of these unseen agencies; and how
to make this felt, how to make it clear and yet not actual, is the problem

of the stage manager. To me it seems that the play has never yet been properly performed because we have never yet felt these spirits working through the woman at the man, and to achieve this would be one of the most difficult tasks which could be set the stage manager, though not because of the difficulty of purchasing gauze which should be sufficiently transparent, not because of the difficulty of finding machinery capable of raising the ghosts, or any other such reason. The chief difficulty lies with the two performers of the roles of Lady Macbeth and Macbeth, for if it is admitted that this spiritual element which Shakespeare called the Witches and Ghosts is in any way connected with the pain of these two beings, Macbeth and his Lady, then these two characters must show this to the audience.

But, while it rests with the actors of these two parts, it also rests with the actors of the witches, and above all with the stage manager, to bring these spirits and their mediums into effective harmony.

On the stage the spirits are never seen during the scenes of Lady Macbeth, neither are we conscious of their influence; yet as we read the play we are not only conscious of the influence of these 'sightless substances'; we are somehow conscious of their presence. We feel it as the presence of the French Abbé was felt in Shorthouse's romance of *The Countess Eve*.

Are there not moments in the play when one of these three spirits seems to have clapped its skinny hand upon Lady Macbeth's mouth and answered in her stead? And who was it, if not one of them, who drew her by the wrist as she passed into the room of the old king with the two daggers in her hand? Who was it pushed her by the elbow as she smeared the faces of the grooms? Again, what is this dagger that Macbeth sees in the air? By what thread of hair does it hang? Who dangles it? And whose is the voice heard as he returns from the chamber of the murdered king?

MACBETH: I've done the deed. Didst thou not hear a noise?
LADY MACBETH: I heard the owl scream and the crickets cry.
    Did not you speak?
MACBETH: When?
LADY MACBETH: Now.
MACBETH: As I descended?

Who is this that was heard to speak as he descended?

And who are these mysterious three who dance gaily without making any sound around this miserable pair as they talk together in the dark after the dark deed? We know quite well as we read; we forget altogether

when we see the play presented upon the stage. There we see only the
weak man being egged on by the ambitious woman who is assuming the
manners of what is called the 'Tragedy Queen'; and in other scenes we
see the same man, having found that the same ambitious lady does not
assist him, calling upon some bogies and having an interview with them
in a cavern.

What we *should* see is a man in that hypnotic state which can be
both terrible and beautiful to witness. We should realise that this hyp-
notism is transmitted to him through the medium of his wife, and we
should recognise the witches as spirits, more terrible because more
beautiful than we can conceive except by making them terrible. We
should see them, not as Hazlitt imagined them, as 'hags of mischief,
obscene panderers to iniquity, malicious from their impotence of enjoy-
ment, enamoured of destruction, because they are themselves unreal,
abortive, half-existences, who become sublime from their exemption
from all human sympathies and contempt for all human affairs', but
rather picture them to ourselves as we picture the militant Christ
scourging the money-lenders, the fools who denied Him. Here we have
the idea of the supreme God, the supreme love, and it is that which has
to be brought into *Macbeth* on the stage. We see in this instance the God
of Force as exemplified in these witches, placing these two pieces of
mortality upon the anvil and crushing them because they were not hard
enough to resist; consuming them because they could not stand the fire:
offering the woman a crown for her husband, flattering her beyond
measure, whispering to her of her superior force, of her superior intellect; whispering to him of his bravery.

See how persuasively the spirits can work upon the man or the woman
when separated and alone! Listen to the flow of their language; they are
drunk with the force of these spirits though unaware of their presence.

But note the moment when these two come together. In each other's
faces they see, as it were, something so strange that they seem to be
surprised by a reminiscence. 'Where have I seen that before or felt that
which I now see?' Each becomes furtive, alert, fearful, on the defensive,
and so there is no outpouring of speech here, but their meeting is like
the cautious approach of two animals.

What is it they see? – the spirit which clings round the feet or hangs
upon the neck, or, as in the old Durer picture, is whispering in the ear?
Yet why, one wonders, should these spirits appear so horrible when a
moment ago we were speaking of them as being so divine as to resemble
the militant Christ? and the answer seems obvious. Is it not possible
that the spirit may take as many forms as the body, as many forms as

thought? These spirits are the many souls of nature, inexorable to the weak, yet obedient to those who obey.

But let us come to the appearance of Banquo at the feast.

The whole play leads up to, and down from, this point. It is here that are pronounced the most terrible words heard during the play, here that is offered the most amazing impression for the eye. And in order to reach this moment decently, intelligently, that is to say, artistically, the figures must not walk about on the ground for the first two acts and suddenly appear on stilts in the third act or line, for then a great truth will appear as a great lie, Banquo's ghost as nothing.

We must open this play high up in an atmosphere loftier than that in which we generally grope, and which is a matter-of-fact, put-on-your-boots atmosphere; for this is a matter of fancy, a matter of that strangely despised thing, the imagination; that which we call the spiritual.

We should be conscious of the desire of the spirit to see the woman utterly annihilated herself rather than submit to the influence which this spirit brings upon the flesh as a test. We should see the horror of the spirit on perceiving the triumph of this influence.

Instead, we see of all this nothing on the stage. We do not know why the witches are worrying these two people; we feel that it is rather unpleasant. But that is not the feeling which should be created in us. We see bogies and imps of the cauldron, and pitchforks, and the little mosquito-like beings of the pantomimes, but we never see the God, the Spirit, which we ought to see; that is to say, the beautiful spirit, that patient, stern being who demands of a hero at least the heroic.

Shakespeare's characters are so often but weak beings; Lady Macbeth is perhaps the weakest of them all, and if that is the beauty – and unmistakably it is a great beauty – it is the beauty of disease and not the supreme beauty.

Having read of these characters, we are left to ourselves and our own contemplation, and each will add that thought which Shakespeare left to be added by each. There is great freedom permitted to the reader, for much has been left unsaid, but so much has also been said that nearly all is indicated, and to the imaginative brain these spirits are clearly implied and the fruits of the imagination are always welcomed by the unimaginative, who devour them as Eve must have devoured the forbidden fruit.

Therefore when a stage manager happens to have imagination he must also set before the people the fruits of this imagination.

But look at the unwieldy material which is tossed to him! What can he do with rubbish such as scenery, such as costumes, such as moving figures which he can shove here and there and place in this or that light? Is this material for so subtle a thing as imagination to work with? Perhaps it is; perhaps it is no worse than marble or the material used for erecting a cathedral; perhaps all depends upon the manner of the use.

Well, then, admitting this, let the stage manager return to the material and determine to shake the dust out of it until he wakens it to real life; that is to say, the life of the imagination. For there is only one real life in art, and that is this life of imagination. The imaginative, that is the real in art, and in no modern play do we see the truth of this so tremendously revealed as in *Macbeth*.

It is all very well for some people to talk about Shakespeare living in a curiously superstitious age, or choosing a theme from an age and a country which was soaked in superstition.

Good heavens! is the idea of a ghost, is the idea of a spirit, so strange? Why, then the whole of Shakespeare is strange and unnatural, and we should hastily burn most of his works, for we want nothing which can be called strange and unnatural in the twentieth century. We want something we can clearly understand, and, as represented upon the stage, these plays are not clear to understand, for the foolish appearance of a spook is not a very understandable thing, though the reality of the presence of spirits around us seems to me to be a thing which all ordinary intelligences should be reminded of.

Yet how can we show this thing properly if we take as the main and primary point for our consideration Macbeth and his wife, Banquo and his horse, and the thrones and the tables, and let these things blind us to the real issues of the drama?

Unless we see these spirits before we begin our work we shall never see them later on. For who can see a spirit by looking for it behind an act drop? No, the man who would show these plays as Shakespeare, perhaps, might wish them to be shown must invest every particle of them with a sense of the spiritual; and to do so he must entirely avoid that which is material, merely rational, or rather, that which exposes only its material shell, for the beholder would then come up against something thick and impenetrable and have to return to that swinging rhythm which flows not only in the *words* of Shakespeare but in his very breath, in the sweet aroma which lingers round his plays.

But to speak more practically in conclusion.

Had I to teach a young man who would venture to achieve this I would act as follows: I would take him through each portion of the play, and from each act, each scene, each thought, action, or sound, I would extract some spirit, the spirit which is there. And on the faces of the actors, on their costumes, and on the scene, by the light, by line, by colour, by movement, voice and every means at our disposal, I would repeatedly and repeatedly bring upon the stage some reminder of the presence of these spirits, so that on the arrival of Banquo's ghost at the feast we should not commence to giggle, but should find it just and terrible; should be so keenly expectant, so attuned to the moment of its coming that we should be conscious of its presence even before we saw it there.

from *Two Letters on Macbeth* (1928). Lady Macbeth

PARAGRAPHS FROM A LETTER ADDRESSED BY THE ARTIST TO THE ACTRESS PLAYING THE ROLE.
To me it seems that Lady M could not be in a room with a group of people without they all began to live with eight times their usual intensity – every one, when she came in, glowed – and, as she went, they went out like electric lights dying down.

She was the centre of a *big* social circle of people – as it is, on the stage we see her the centre of a circle of five hand-maidens – two butlers – a messenger and a lot of awkward spear bearers – and what is that for us?

A second thing: It seemed to me that, although the centre of it all, she never *appeared* in the centre – she hugged the sides, her eyes alone focus the centre and there, she saw to it, stood husband – a man with some poetic fancy in his speech, but a quite dull and awkward, melancholy sort of creature – with a knack of strength – physical.

The play seems to me always to suffer in representation because we see *two centre* figures.

I would have it – if possible – one centre *dull* and the other always hugging the walls *vivid*.

Before five minutes our minds would be asking, 'this man – this boor – what is he? What's he so much in evidence for? Why is he here at all?' – and before another three minutes were gone we should be searching the shadows for his reason – i.e., Lady M. We should from then onwards be ALERT – we should be waiting breathlessly to catch the glint of her eyes – and when she did ever advance, we should long for her to stay, so attractive she is; and yet always she goes.

Is something like this possible with you? I don't know how it is, but she seems to me pretty rather than handsome; *seductive* rather than

compelling; in fact *I cannot find her even once compelling* in the masculine
sense of the word. She seems to have Bernhardt's voice when Bernhardt
was talking to Armand in *La Dame aux C*. Are we agreed? I cannot hear
her calling on 'All ye spirits' in the voice of Siddons – but in the voice
of *Camille* gone a bit crazy.

Drunken if you will, but not devastating – What 'Spirit' that she calls on
ever came to any one in response to an order thrilled with mere intensity –
but a spirit might be wooed. It is just possible. – Are we agreed?

Can you speak such a passage with your eyelids covering your eyes? –
in ecstasy – sensual – immense?

But to answer questions.

I had planned a scene for your first entrance: with a small room,
little door – bolts – key – bed (no fireplace, alas!) – the messenger to
knock, *not* blurt in – unordered.

Have no thoughts of murder exactly in your head and no feelings of
that when you greet that company of guests – why bother about *that* –
time for that. . . .

Scene before banquet.

Don't let them hamper you with a scrap more material, cloth, brass,
gold, or cloaks than you feel attractive in – be *that* to the full, I beg of
you, and one-half the troubles of this play are removed.

A different beauty – Don't be too *erect* – bend – listen, not with
straight head, but with head well cocked on one side – at M when he's
murdering I mean: it's almost jaunty she is: 'how easy is't'. She almost
drawls charmingly. I'd not even oblige you to wear a big cloak. Select
the loveliest grey and grey-white furs for some part of Act I, and the
loveliest pieces of gold fine spun stuff for Act II–III – the Indian gold
cloth is good.

Did it ever occur to you to dress up in a more or less modern dress –
I'm not ignorant of the latest 1928 thing, but I mean those swathing
dresses of 1913 or thereabouts.

You don't want to *force* the modern, but you *could* let it slip out
couldn't you? and thus make one feel the woman was a reality.

Don't laugh – because though I know I am rather a good stage
manager, I am quite aware already that I know *nothing* about ladies'
dresses – so you mustn't laugh.

By the way. . . .

Where a setting doesn't seem to feel right to you, I beg of you not to
bother about it. Settings are of NO ACCOUNT, scenery is rubbish,
they never have been or will be of account, where an actress is there to
attract.

If you attract (plus the bit of makeup and scarf and rings to explain that you ARE LADY MACBETH) no one will even look at what scene you are in.

I have not been able to give you my big staircase in the sleep-walking scene – get my book *Towards a New Theatre*, and flatter me by looking at that design. It's not bad for me.

But I have given you, a stairway. [See illustration 22.]

Pillar

⟨...?   enters here
⟨...?   a halting place
⟨...?   scene for sleep-walking
Exits here....⟩

Now I am afraid I may horrify you by the drawing I've made of Lady M herself during her sleep-walking – and which has gone to Mr Tyler along with the other designs. Because it's ugly. It makes her ugly – it makes her untidy – she slops along in straw slippers, slipped into night after night. She is not impressive, she is merely almost daft and uncouth.

I've seen a woman of forty-five – grey, old-looking as eighty, walking as in sleep or plodding along – voice *husky* as that of a drunken man – growling continually like a dog: TRAGIC as a Shakespeare thing is tragic: As a Japanese ghost picture is tragic: ... get some to look at.

And if I saw such a perfectly enchanting woman like Lady Macbeth of Act I changed to a horror of Act IV, I should feel I was looking at something Shakespearean.

from *Foreword to The Theatre Advancing* (1921)

Someone tells me that I have written elsewhere that Shakespeare's plays are not for acting – Can I have contradicted myself? Oh, what a sin! Can I have said that you can say '*Yes*' and '*No*' and yet reply correctly. If I have not said so you know quite well that this is true – that *under some conditions* 'Yes' is the only reply to make to a question to which 'No' is the sole answer.

Let me ask you to be a little more cautious before asserting that I contradict myself – for here I happen not to. When I spoke of Shakespeare as being not actable, not for the stage, I spoke, if you will remember, as one who was reviewing the whole question of the theatre of the world – and the theatre as a creative art. Here I speak as one who reviews one section of the whole – the most backward section – that is, the English theatre. And for the English theatre it will do well – can do no better – to begin at Shakespeare. For in Shakespeare is all *Burbage* remember; in Shakespeare is a huge deposit of the *Commedia dell'arte*.

You who fail to understand how I can make two such apparently contradictory statements about the Shakespearean plays would fail to understand that a paradox covers the whole truth. If you cannot understand that Shakespeare's plays are unactable and yet are the best stuff on which to rebuild the English theatre of 1920 – then you cannot understand a paradox.

from *Index to the Story of My Days* (1957)

An odd word 'impossible'. I was one of the Impossibles – and became in time one of the leaders of (a section of) that vast crowd. The impossibles are the impenitent independents: the true rebels – they who come to rebel because born to do so.

We Impossibles see ghosts – have stepfathers – develop a sense of humour – love frantically – have mothers. We all, when young, thought well of ourselves, somewhat critically of each other and didn't like the rest. An Impossible would often become the firm friend of another Impossible. Now and again two impossibles would fall in love with each other – and very seriously too . . . jesting at themselves all the time – *nearly* all the time.

We Impossibles felt (and so we *knew*) we were gifted beings – useless to the world, for the world was unable to appreciate or employ us, to pay or feed us. People were always asking us to be practical; they wanted us to stop being ourselves quite so markedly; not to be continually doing things, wearing things, suggesting or doing. And we did things right enough. No one would admit it until one of us trumpeted our little deeds aloud.

Those who disliked us intensely never ceased to decry us – apparently because our crimes were not their crimes, and they were always complaining that we were not quick enough in our *technique*. Said they: 'You are fools – you don't know how to pick a pocket – or cheat at cards – or lie like truth: you are floundering – you are not quick enough at it – you fumble and give the whole art away.'

So they said – and I suppose they really looked on roguery as an art and as the one and only art. Mind you, they had a real *knowledge of* the world: we only guessed at it. We certainly fumbled in our technique. When we tried to pick a handkerchief out of a lady's pocket, we more

often than not began by searching our own sleeves for an ace or a king
– we mixed up the several crafts!

There are Impossibles in every land – as I came to discover when I
travelled: but I write here of England – London – and of the years
between 1880 and 1905. We English Impossibles were of the clan to
which Hamlet belonged; and Hamlet is only different from others because he lacks *technique* and advancement – a sense of business. He
thinks aloud, whereas the rogues don't. If they think at all they conceal
their thoughts – and how wise of them! Hamlet suspects foul play – not
here or there but everywhere – and everyone at last comes to see this;
but they all agree that technically he should not do so; nor seem to see
ghosts or hear voices; it's not done – certainly not in a Court. Hamlet
tries to win the sincere regard and affection of each one of the people
in Elsinore; and they all think this shows very bad taste on his part. It
may show good feeling, but who bothers about feeling. Court technique
is the thing and Hamlet seems to put no value on that. He's quite
impossible! Besides Hamlet is idle – he reads a lot – but he *does* nothing!
If he had to make his own living, he would soon be on the rocks. He is
an idle good-for-nothing! His uncle Claudius, on the other hand, is a
good man. He was a man who, seeing his elder brother had made a
mess of the Elsinore accounts – (he was always sleeping in the orchard
when he should have been in the office and at work) – did what all
good men do – 'took the bull by the horns' – and, after a few neat
technical operations, took over the laborious job as indicated by Shakespeare and got things going within two months. A really efficient, first-
class man was Claudius – no one could possibly criticise such a man. It
was, people thought, just a little too much of a good thing that such a
man as Claudius should have a weak-minded stepson (the very Prince
of Denmark) everlastingly yapping at his heels.

Now, we Impossibles of 1900 resembled this same Prince of Denmark
– and the world around us did, said, felt, and thought about us exactly
as did the Court at Elsinore.

Last Words

Romantic to the last Craig's apology for his life as an 'impossible' is a little sad, written, as it was, in *Index to the Story of My Days*. The year he was writing about was 1903 but the book was not published until 1957. It may well be that this entry was barely edited from a daybook reference of 1903 when he was thirty-one years old. More probably, alas, he still thought of himself as a Hamlet figure at the age of eighty-five.

Edward Gordon Craig seems to have been an odd mixture. 'A cantankerous old rebel' Sir John Gielgud called him when introducing the exhibition at the Victoria and Albert Museum, yet the affection and respect in which he held his cousin are undeniable. Craig's son Edward recalls the pleasure the old man took in the reprint in 1962 of *On The Art of the Theatre*, not so much because some of his writings were again in print but because the book was described as a source of 'inspiration, anger and delight': anger in particular. 'It's good for them to feel angry. It makes them do things.'

He had visitors in the last years at Vence but the visits must have seemed rare oases in a desert of inaction. Letters were often filled with melancholy and if loneliness in age is a burden to which our early lives contribute, the accumulated frustration of a lifetime in art is an added load which genius does not deserve to bear.

In 1959 when Kenneth Tynan interviewed him for *The Observer* he saw no signs of bitterness or apathy and plenty of indication that, if the world were not keeping up with Craig, at least Craig was keeping up with the world. The last words of the article he wrote for *The Observer* on his return make a fitting tribute to the first theorist of the modern British theatre. 'I took my leave exhausted, though he was not. . . . The theatre is not yet ripe for Gordon Craig. Perhaps, indeed, it never will be. But, meanwhile, at Vence, work is still in progress. When the theatrical millennium arrives, he will be its first harbinger and surest witness.'

Conclusion

My last word will be a plea.

Be a little more careful, I beg you, not to misrepresent me and my friends to the people. We have chosen a difficult, not the easiest way. Have we shirked any discomfort and any sacrifices that were to be made for our theatre? Have we more to sacrifice? . . . only say so and we can attempt it. But don't misrepresent us. Century after century we are always the same . . . you must say that we are faithful.

You get cross with us sometimes for nothing.

If we say we want applause to cease in theatres you don't give it a moment's thought and you fail to give the matter careful investigation. If you thought and enquired you would find that the very people whom you imagine love applause, hate it. If you are a member of society you applaud a celebrated Jenny Lind and set her up as your example of how a public favourite feels about such things . . . for you think she adores it. But Princess Pauline Metternich tells us in her memoirs that Jenny Lind at the end of a song, when the applause was frantic, raised her hand saying 'Please don't applaud. I have always disliked applause and fuss and it was to avoid them that I left the stage so soon.'

If you are a socialist you applaud the name of Mazzini just as crowds once applauded the man. 'Absurd applause,' says Mazzini himself of the custom.

And if you will only think a while longer and enquire into the past you will find most of my proposals in this book are reasonable, and that many of them can be found put into practice, or longed to be practised, by the best of our fellow workers in the past: by the great names you justly honour.

And so it would be an easy matter – and a reasonable one – to put them once more into practice.

Whereas, the proposals which are new – the hints I give to bring us a new theatre, – these need not so much your thought or careful enquiry as your courage. Courage to accept them . . . for it is only your fear which causes you to reject them and so to lose something . . . and courage to urge that they be put immediately into practice. Show courage towards me and you do no harm and much good to the people and most of all to yourself.

For if you do not show courage in this, my ideas will die with me – for no one but myself can possibly carry them into execution. Of this I am quite sure.

And you – are you not beginning to suspect it too? You thought ten years ago that any young and intelligent and enthusiastic follower of mine could be persuaded, encouraged, and paid to bring out 'Craig's ideas' as they are called.

Reinhardt comes: you thought you had the ideas then – and cheaply. The Russian Ballet: – you still think they brought you something of the kind . . . and hardly a month passes but some new and crazy adventurer appears in Rome, in Paris, London or New Yoek and you nudge yourself and fancy you are going to get my ideas at last – and cheaply – and without obligation to me.

But you are not beginning to see that you are no nearer the solution – and that the problem you thought so easy is not to be solved until you turn to me and empower me to solve it in whatever way seems best to me?

And I think you know by this time that I will only show my work in future in a theatre of my own.

I was five to six times asked by Reinhardt to enter his admirable theatre and produce a play as I wish to see it produced. I did not do so – and I will do no such thing. 'What, you won't produce a play as you wish to see it produced!' . . . I seem to hear the scream. Calmly, please. I never said any such bosh. I said I will not enter another man's theatre and do it. I will do it only in my own theatre. Is that clear? Do you know the old song beginning 'Will you walk into my parlour . . .'?

You are strange people. You blame me for not taking into their theatres the very things which I am keeping for you so that you may have them intact in mine. In their theatres the ideas would be pulled limb from limb. Is it not so? – and what are they worth in pieces? You see what they are worth for you have them in pieces: . . . yet your public raves over them – that's the queerest thing of all. Yes, you are a strange people.

You don't go on in that way about paintings, do you? Perhaps you do

– but it seemed to me that when you are purchasing paintings for the National Gallery you're very careful to buy an original, a genuine Bellini, or an authentic Van Dyck. I never heard of the National Gallery preferring to purchase AN IMITATION of one of the panels of a triptych by Memling to the genuine three panels. Did you? And yet that's exactly the whole English policy in regard to nearly all theatrical works of art. If it *can* get the imitation it seems delighted. 'The original was too expensive' is the feeble reply which is nearly always offered. Which is obviously only the excuse vamped up in the confusion of the moment when the purchasers see what a hash they've made of the whole transaction.

And now, because I have not given you a text book called 'Craig's ideas, and how to put each one of them into practice', do not misrepresent the book and me by saying that I am unpractical.

If I haven't given you the whole of my ideas the modern theatre holds proof that I've given you some, and that these are put into execution.

I give you some more here. Don't be churlish and ask with some show of a grievance why I've not given you all. I think it's your turn to do something.

The attempt to antagonise the artist by throwing ever one more obstacle in his path:

(A) By rejecting what he has to bring; by doing this beyond the regulation time limit;
(B) by supporting one foreigner the more;
(C) by not empowering him to work;
(D) by criticising the work they have not seen;
(E) by praising turpitudes;
(F) and by numerous other methods the which roll away from my mind like the famous water does off the infamous duck's back . . .

this attempt to antagonise him does succeed – for a short while. And it is necessary to his progress that this be so.

But as it does not succeed in doing *more* than this – and since he merely resorts to blockade – and you get no genuine goods into England – is it wise to fool away the time turning the artist into Aunt Sally . . . and failing to hit him every time?

Who would not willingly serve as so British a figure to real sportsmen: but I ask myself, is this sort of thing real sport? is it playing the game? . . . and I leave you to answer what concerns me no longer.

Appendix

Productions for which Craig was responsible as designer, director, or both.

December 1893 London, Uxbridge Town Hall: Alfred de Musset *No Trifling with Love*.

July 1896 London, Parkhurst Theatre: Shakespeare *Hamlet* and *Romeo and Juliet*, playing leads in both.

January 1897 Croydon, Theatre Royal: Wilkie Collins *The New Magdalen* and S.X. Courte *François Villon*.

May 1900 London, Hampstead Conservatoire: Henry Purcell *Dido and Aeneas*, with Martin Shaw.

March 1901 London, Coronet Theatre: *Dido and Aeneas* and *The Masque of Love* (from Purcell's *Dioclesian*), with Martin Shaw.

March 1902 London, Great Queen Street Theatre: Handel and John Gay *Acis and Galatea* and *The Masque of Love*, with Martin Shaw.

December 1902 London, Imperial Institute: Laurence Housman *Bethlehem*, with Martin Shaw.

January 1903 London, Shaftesbury Theatre: R. G. Legge *For Sword or Song* for Julia Neilson and Fred Terry. 'EGC is given Act I, Scene I to deal with – and last act.'

April 1903 London, Imperial Theatre: Ibsen *The Vikings*, under the management of Ellen Terry.

May 1903 London, Imperial Theatre: Shakespeare *Much Ado About Nothing*, under the management of Ellen Terry.

January 1905 Berlin, Lessing Theatre: Thomas Otway *Das Gerettete Venedig* (*Venice Preserved*), with designs by Craig (modified).

December 1906 Florence, Pergola Theatre: Ibsen *Rosmersholm*, with designs by Craig (modified), for Eleanora Duse.

January 1911 Dublin, Abbey Theatre: Lady Gregory *The Deliverer* and W. B. Yeats *The Hour Glass*. First use of Craig's 'screens'.

January 1912 Moscow, Arts Theatre: Shakespeare *Hamlet*, '. . . produced by me with Mr Stanislavsky's assistance . . .'.

November 1926 Copenhagen, Royal Theatre: Ibsen *Kongs-Emnerne* (*The Pretenders*) with Adam and Johannes Poulsen.

November 1928   New York, Knickerbocker Theatre: Shakespeare *Macbeth*, with designs based on Craig's ideas (designs signed C.p.b. 'Craig-potboilers').

Bibliography

By Craig.

Edward Gordon Craig, a bibliography by Ifan Kyrle Fletcher and Arnold Rood (see below) is the definitive guide to all that Craig designed and published. The following selection of major works draws heavily upon that admirable piece of scholarship, identifying usually first editions in English only.

The Page. Ed. periodical Vols I to IV. Hackbridge, At the Sign of the Rose, 1898–1901.

Gordon Craig's Book of Penny Toys. Hackbridge, At the Sign of the Rose, 1899.

Henry Irving, Ellen Terry etc.; a book of portraits. Chicago, H. S. Stone and Co, 1899.

Bookplates. Hackbridge, At the Sign of the Rose, 1900.

The Art of the Theatre: together with an introduction by Edward Gordon Craig and a preface by R. Graham Robertson. Edinburgh and London, T. N. Foulis, 1905.

The Mask. Ed. periodical Vols I to XV. Florence, 1908–29. Craig also contributed a majority of the articles and reviews under his own name, and, by his own admission, sixty-six pseudonyms.

A Portfolio of Etchings. Florence, 1908.

On the Art of the Theatre. London, William Heinemann, 1911.

W. B. Yeats: Plays for an Irish Theatre with designs by Gordon Craig. London and Stratford-upon-Avon, A. H. Bullen, 1911.

Towards a New Theatre. London and Toronto, J. M. Dent and Sons Ltd, 1913.

A Living Theatre: The Gordon Craig School. Florence, School of the Art of the Theatre, 1913.

The Marionnette. Ed. periodical Vol I nos 1 to 12. Florence, Box 444, 1918–19.

The Drama for Fools by Tom Fool: five motions for marionnettes, published individually as *Mr Fish and Mrs Bones, The Tune the Old Cow Died of, The Gordian Knot, The Three Men of Gotham, Romeo and Juliet.* Florence, 1918.

The Theatre Advancing. Boston, Little, Brown and Company, 1919.

Scene. London, Humphrey Milford Oxford University Press, 1923.

Woodcuts and Some Words. London and Toronto, J. M. Dent and Sons Ltd, 1924.

Nothing or The Bookplate. London, J. M. Dent and Sons Ltd, 1924.

Books and Theatres. London and Toronto, J. M. Dent and Sons Ltd, 1925.

Henry Irving. London, J. M. Dent and Sons Ltd, 1930.

William Shakespeare: The Tragedie of Hamlet Prince of Denmarke. Weimar, The Cranach Press, 1930.

A Production: being thirty-two collotype plates of designs projected or realised for The Pretenders of Henrik Ibsen and produced at the Royal Theatre Copenhagen 1926 by Edward Gordon Craig. London, Oxford University Press Humphrey Milford, 1930.

Fourteen Notes. Seattle, University of Washington Bookstore, 1931.

Ellen Terry and her Secret Self. London, Sampson Low, Marston and Co Ltd, 1931.

Index to the Story of My Days. London, Hulton Press, 1957.

Edward Gordon Craig: radio talks, extracts from a diary, woodcuts. Three records and engravings. London, Discurio, 1962.

The Life and Strange Surprising Adventures of Robinson Crusoe of York (Craig-Defoe): illustrated by Edward Gordon Craig, introduced by Edward A. Craig. London, Basilisk Press, 1979.

About Craig.

Bablet, Denis. *Edward Gordon Craig.* Paris, L'Arche, 1962. Translated by Daphne Woodward: London, Heinemann Educational Books Ltd, 1966. Reissued as *The Theatre of Edward Gordon Craig* London, Eyre Methuen Ltd, 1981.

Craig, Edward. *Gordon Craig: the story of his life.* London, Victor Gollancz Ltd, 1968.

Craig, Edward. *Edward Gordon Craig: The Last Eight Years.* Andoversford, The Whittington Press, 1983.

Fletcher, Ifan Kyrle and Rood, Arthur. *Edward Gordon Craig: a bibliography.* London, Society for Theatre Research, 1967.

Johnson, Albert E. *Catalogue of an exhibition of the work of Edward Gordon Craig.* Memphis, State University Library, 1970.

Leeper, Janet. *Edward Gordon Craig: designs for the theatre.* Harmondsworth, Penguin Books, 1948.

Marker, Frederick J. and Lise-Lone. *Edward Gordon Craig and The Pretenders: a production revisited.* Carbondale and Edwardsville, Southern Illinois University Press, 1981.

Marotti, Feruccio. *Edward Gordon Craig.* Bologna, Cappelli, 1961.

Nash, George. *Edward Gordon Craig 1872–1966.* London, Her Majesty's Stationery Office, 1967.

Newman, L. M. *Gordon Craig Archives.* London, The Malkin Press, 1976.

Rood, Arthur. *Edward Gordon Craig: artist of the theatre 1872–1966.* Exhibition catalogue with an introduction by Donald Oenslager. New York, The New York Public Library, 1967.

Rood, Arthur. *Gordon Craig on Movement and Dance.* London, Dance Books, 1977.

Rose, Enid. *Gordon Craig and the Theatre*. London, Sampson Low, Marston and Co Ltd, 1931.

Senelick, Laurence. *Gordon Craig's Moscow Hamlet: a reconstruction*. Westport, Greenwood Press, 1982.

Steegmuller, Francis, ed. *'Your Isadora': the love story of Isadora Duncan and Gordon Craig*. London, Macmillan, 1974.

Valogne, Catherine. *Gordon Craig*. Paris, Les Presses Littéraires de France, 1953.

WITHDRAWN

Acknowledgements

I have received assistance from a number of people in the preparation of this book. I should like to record my special thanks to Craig's son, Edward Craig, and to George Nash, for the considerable help they gave me in tracking down sources. Also to Sir John Gielgud, Sir Bernard Miles and Arnold Rood for approving the choice of material, to H. E. Robert Craig, administrator of the Edward Gordon Craig Estate, and to Gillian Jason of the Gillian Jason Gallery for allowing photographs of her exhibition. These photographs were taken by my colleague Tony Meech, to whom I am indebted for the preparation of visual material, and for reading and advising on the whole manuscript.

For permission to publish extracts from Edward Gordon Craig's writings, acknowledgement is made to the following: for the extract from *Woodcuts and Some Words* (1924); *Literary Theatres* (1908); *The Perishable Theatre* (1921); *A Note on Masks* (1910); *Gentlemen, The Marionnette* (1908); *Candlelight* (1922); *Proposals Old and New* (1910); extract from *Rearrangements* (1915); *Theatrical Reform* (1910); extract from *A Production* (1930); extract from *An International Symposium* (1904); *Theatre and English Theatre* (1924); extracts from *Scene* (1923); extracts from *Index to the Story of My Days* (1957); extract from *Henry Irving* (1930); extract from *A Letter to Ellen Terry* (1908); extract from *The Artists of the Theatre of the Future* (1908); extract from *The Actor and the Über-Marionnette* (1907); extract from *A Durable Theatre* (1921); *Stanislavsky's System* (1937); extract from *To Feel or Not to Feel* (1924); extract from *Thoroughness in the Theatre* (1911); *On Learning Magic* (1921); extract from *A Letter to Ellen Terry* (1917); *Enter the Army* (1900); *The Arrival* (1901); *The Steps 1, 2, 3, 4* (1905); *Study for Movement* (1906); *A Study for Movement* (1906); *A Palace, a Slum and a Stairway* (1907); extract from *The Old School of Acting* (1915); extract from *The Thousand Scenes in One Scene* (1915); *Shakespeare's Collaborators* (1913); *Shakespeare's Plays* (1908); *On 'The Tempest'* (1924); extract from *The Artists of the Theatre of the Future* (1907); *On the Ghosts* in the Tragedies of Shakespeare (1908); *Two Letters on 'Macbeth'* (1929); extracts from Foreword to *The Theatre Advancing* (1921); to H. E. Robert Craig: copyright in all these extracts by the Edward Gordon Craig Estate; for the extracts from *The Art of the Theatre. The First Dialogue* and *The Art of the Theatre. The Second Dialogue*, to William Heinemann Ltd., London (from *On The Art of the Theatre*, 1911).